The
CATHOLIC
CHURCH

OPPOSING VIEWPOINTS®

Other Books of Related Interest

OPPOSING VIEWPOINTS SERIES

Abortion
Child Abuse
Culture Wars
The Family
Homosexuality
Religion in America
Sex

CURRENT CONTROVERSIES SERIES

The Abortion Controversy
Homosexuality

AT ISSUE SERIES

Anti-Semitism
Child Sexual Abuse in the Catholic Church
The Ethics of Abortion
Gay and Lesbian Families
Gay Marriage
Is American Culture in Decline?
Religion and Education
Reproductive Technology
Sex Education
Should Abortion Rights Be Restricted?

The CATHOLIC CHURCH

OPPOSING VIEWPOINTS®

Mary E. Williams, *Book Editor*

Bruce Glassman, *Vice President*
Bonnie Szumski, *Publisher*
Helen Cothran, *Managing Editor*

OPPOSING
VIEWPOINTS®
SERIES

GREENHAVEN PRESS
An imprint of Thomson Gale, a part of The Thomson Corporation

THOMSON
™
GALE

Detroit • New York • San Francisco • San Diego • New Haven, Conn.
Waterville, Maine • London • Munich

THOMSON

✴ ™
GALE

LIBRARY OF CONGRESS CATALOGING-IN-PUBLICATION DATA

The Catholic Church / Mary E. Williams, book editor.
    p. cm. — (Opposing viewpoints series)
Includes bibliographical references and index.
ISBN 0-7377-3229-6 (lib. : alk. paper) — ISBN 0-7377-3230-X (pbk. : alk. paper)
    1. Catholic Church. I. Williams, Mary E., 1960– . II. Opposing viewpoints series (Unnumbered)
BX880.C275 2006
282—dc22
                                                                        2005046115

Printed in the United States of America

"Congress shall make
no law...abridging the
freedom of speech, or of
the press."

First Amendment to the U.S. Constitution

The basic foundation of our democracy is the First
Amendment guarantee of freedom of expression.
The Opposing Viewpoints Series is dedicated to the
concept of this basic freedom and the idea that it is
more important to practice it than to enshrine it.

Contents

Why Consider Opposing Viewpoints?   9

Introduction   12

Chapter 1: What Is the State of the Catholic Church?

Chapter Preface   16

1. The Sex Abuse Scandal Has Caused Lasting Damage to the Church   18
   James K. Fitzpatrick

2. The Sex Abuse Scandal Has Not Caused Lasting Damage to the Church   23
   Richard P. McBrien

3. The Papacy of John Paul II Was a Success   27
   Jeffrey Fleishman

4. The Papacy of John Paul II Was Deeply Flawed   31
   Andrew Sullivan

5. The Catholic Church Has Not Acknowledged Its Anti-Semitism   36
   Daniel Jonah Goldhagen

6. Charges of Catholic Anti-Semitism Have Been Exaggerated   46
   David G. Dalin

7. Progressive Reformers Are Pushing for Institutional Change   55
   Angela Bonavoglia

8. Observant Youths Are Returning to Established Traditions   64
   Bronwen Catherine McShea

Periodical Bibliography   70

Chapter 2: What Led to the Sex Abuse Scandal in the Catholic Church?

Chapter Preface   72

1. Homosexuality in the Priesthood Contributes to Child Sexual Abuse   74
   Rod Dreher

2. Homosexuality in the Priesthood Does Not
   Contribute to Child Sexual Abuse   83
   Thomas J. Gumbleton

3. The Celibacy Requirement for Priests Fosters
   Child Sexual Abuse   92
   Sarah McCarthy

4. The Celibacy Requirement for Priests Does
   Not Foster Child Sexual Abuse   101
   Philip Jenkins

5. A Culture of Dissent Contributes to Child
   Sexual Abuse   107
   George Weigel

6. A Culture of Secrecy Contributes to Child
   Sexual Abuse   115
   Larry B. Stammer

Periodical Bibliography   122

Chapter 3: Should the Catholic Church Try to Influence Politics and Culture?

Chapter Preface   124

1. The Church Should Deny Communion to Catholic
   Politicians Who Oppose Church Teachings   126
   John Donoghue, Robert Baker, and Peter Jugis

2. The Church Should Not Deny Communion
   to Catholic Politicians Who Oppose Church
   Teachings   130
   Joan Chittister

3. The Catholic Church Should Oppose Homosexual
   Marriage   135
   Congregation for the Doctrine of the Faith

4. The Catholic Church Should Not Oppose
   Homosexual Marriage   141
   Matthew Fox

5. The Catholic Church Should Continue to Oppose
   Artificial Contraception   146
   Catholic Insight

6. The Catholic Church's Opposition to Condom
   Use Is Immoral   152
   Katha Pollitt

Periodical Bibliography   157

**Chapter 4: Should the Catholic Church Be
   Reformed?**

Chapter Preface   159

1. The Catholic Church Should Become More
   Democratic   161
   Eugene C. Bianchi

2. The Catholic Church Should Not Become More
   Democratic   167
   New Oxford Review

3. Priestly Celibacy Should Be Optional   173
   Richard Rohr

4. Priestly Celibacy Should Not Be Optional   178
   Frank Morriss

5. Women Should Be Ordained as Priests   184
   Women's Ordination Conference

6. Women Should Not Be Ordained as Priests   192
   Mary Jo Anderson

Periodical Bibliography   201

Glossary   202
For Further Discussion   204
Organizations to Contact   206
Bibliography of Books   213
Index   215

Why Consider Opposing Viewpoints?

"The only way in which a human being can make some approach to knowing the whole of a subject is by hearing what can be said about it by persons of every variety of opinion and studying all modes in which it can be looked at by every character of mind. No wise man ever acquired his wisdom in any mode but this."

John Stuart Mill

In our media-intensive culture it is not difficult to find differing opinions. Thousands of newspapers and magazines and dozens of radio and television talk shows resound with differing points of view. The difficulty lies in deciding which opinion to agree with and which "experts" seem the most credible. The more inundated we become with differing opinions and claims, the more essential it is to hone critical reading and thinking skills to evaluate these ideas. Opposing Viewpoints books address this problem directly by presenting stimulating debates that can be used to enhance and teach these skills. The varied opinions contained in each book examine many different aspects of a single issue. While examining these conveniently edited opposing views, readers can develop critical thinking skills such as the ability to compare and contrast authors' credibility, facts, argumentation styles, use of persuasive techniques, and other stylistic tools. In short, the Opposing Viewpoints Series is an ideal way to attain the higher-level thinking and reading skills so essential in a culture of diverse and contradictory opinions.

In addition to providing a tool for critical thinking, Opposing Viewpoints books challenge readers to question their own strongly held opinions and assumptions. Most people form their opinions on the basis of upbringing, peer pressure, and personal, cultural, or professional bias. By reading carefully balanced opposing views, readers must directly confront new ideas as well as the opinions of those with whom they disagree. This is not to simplistically argue that everyone who reads opposing views will—or should—change his or her opinion. Instead, the series enhances readers' understanding of their own views by encouraging confrontation with opposing ideas. Careful examination of others' views can lead to the readers' understanding of the logical inconsistencies in their own opinions, perspective on why they hold an opinion, and the consideration of the possibility that their opinion requires further evaluation.

Evaluating Other Opinions

To ensure that this type of examination occurs, Opposing Viewpoints books present all types of opinions. Prominent spokespeople on different sides of each issue as well as well-known professionals from many disciplines challenge the reader. An additional goal of the series is to provide a forum for other, less known, or even unpopular viewpoints. The opinion of an ordinary person who has had to make the decision to cut off life support from a terminally ill relative, for example, may be just as valuable and provide just as much insight as a medical ethicist's professional opinion. The editors have two additional purposes in including these less known views. One, the editors encourage readers to respect others' opinions—even when not enhanced by professional credibility. It is only by reading or listening to and objectively evaluating others' ideas that one can determine whether they are worthy of consideration. Two, the inclusion of such viewpoints encourages the important critical thinking skill of objectively evaluating an author's credentials and bias. This evaluation will illuminate an author's reasons for taking a particular stance on an issue and will aid in readers' evaluation of the author's ideas.

It is our hope that these books will give readers a deeper understanding of the issues debated and an appreciation of the complexity of even seemingly simple issues when good and honest people disagree. This awareness is particularly important in a democratic society such as ours in which people enter into public debate to determine the common good. Those with whom one disagrees should not be regarded as enemies but rather as people whose views deserve careful examination and may shed light on one's own.

Thomas Jefferson once said that "difference of opinion leads to inquiry, and inquiry to truth." Jefferson, a broadly educated man, argued that "if a nation expects to be ignorant and free . . . it expects what never was and never will be." As individuals and as a nation, it is imperative that we consider the opinions of others and examine them with skill and discernment. The Opposing Viewpoints Series is intended to help readers achieve this goal.

David L. Bender and Bruno Leone,
Founders

Greenhaven Press anthologies primarily consist of previously published material taken from a variety of sources, including periodicals, books, scholarly journals, newspapers, government documents, and position papers from private and public organizations. These original sources are often edited for length and to ensure their accessibility for a young adult audience. The anthology editors also change the original titles of these works in order to clearly present the main thesis of each viewpoint and to explicitly indicate the opinion presented in the viewpoint. These alterations are made in consideration of both the reading and comprehension levels of a young adult audience. Every effort is made to ensure that Greenhaven Press accurately reflects the original intent of the authors included in this anthology.

Introduction

"The [Catholic] Church stands at a precarious point at the turn of the millennium."

—*Donald B. Cozzens*

With at least one billion Catholics in the world—and an estimated 63 million in the United States alone—Catholicism is one of the world's most renowned faith traditions. Its broad inclusion of people from widely varying cultures, classes, and political affiliations suggests that the Catholic Church is a uniquely dynamic, multifaceted religious institution. Lately, many observers maintain, it is also perhaps the most troubled Christian denomination, plagued with scandal, internal conflict, and a distressing shortage of priests—particularly in North America, where there has been a marked decline in the number of priests over the past four decades. In the United States, for example, the total number of priests dropped by fifteen thousand between 1965 and 2003. New ordinations have also fallen—from 994 in 1965, to 533 in 1985, to 441 in 2003. At the same time, the overall Catholic population has increased by nearly 20 million since 1965. The impact that the decline of priests has had on American Catholic churches is significant: Today there are more than three thousand U.S. parishes with no resident priest, in comparison to 549 such parishes in 1965. In addition, there are more priests over ninety than there are priests under thirty.

While lay people, administrators, and deacons have taken on more of the responsibilities of managing the church, the priesthood remains vitally important to a religion that emphasizes sacred rites. In Catholicism, priests are required for the proper administration of sacraments, most notably the central sacrament of eucharist (holy communion) which occurs at each Mass. A noticeable consequence of the decline in priests is that U.S. Catholics, particularly those in rural regions, have limited access to their denomination's celebration of communion.

One major factor bearing on the clerical shortage, many argue, is the question of mandatory clerical celibacy.

Catholicism is the only branch of Christianity that prohibits priests from marrying or engaging in sexual activity. According to the Corps of Reserved Priests United for Service (CORPUS), during the past four decades an estimated twenty-five thousand priests left active ministry to marry. While some have joined other denominations, CORPUS believes that 50 percent of married ex-priests would be willing to return to Catholic ministry if invited. Moreover, a sizable majority of U.S. Catholics—73 percent—favor allowing priests the option of marriage. Thus, church authorities are facing ever-increasing demands to drop celibacy as a requirement for the priesthood.

Celibacy was not demanded of disciples and clerics in the earliest days of Christianity. In the New Testament the evangelist Paul promoted celibacy for those who could embrace it but also conceded that it was a gift not granted to everyone: "It is a good thing for [the unmarried and the widows] to remain as they are, as I do, but if they cannot exercise self-control they should marry, for it is better to marry than to be on fire" (that is, to sin by having sex outside of marriage). By the late third century, however, priestly celibacy began to be enforced, although it was not uniformly practiced. This enforcement was rooted in the belief that a priest needed to be spiritually focused to administer sacraments and therefore should abstain from sex the night before celebrating a Mass. As Mass increasingly became a daily ritual, permanent celibacy became the norm. Still, the apparently inconsistent observance of celibacy brought scandal to the church. Fearing that the offspring of priests could undermine Catholicism's economic base by acquiring church lands through inheritance, Pope Benedict VIII (1012–1024) enacted laws to protect church property, and subsequent popes reemphasized the rules on clerical celibacy. By 1100, a period of reform had ushered in a more consistent observance of this obligation. The Council of Trent (1545–1563) upheld the value of priestly celibacy but also acknowledged that mandatory celibacy was a church rule rather than a divine rule. Thus, Catholic bishops concluded, the law regarding clerical celibacy could be changed should the church deem it necessary.

Those opposed to the celibacy requirement claim that the

law excludes many gifted and dedicated men who would serve the Church admirably. As Sister Fran Ferder and Father John Heagle of Seattle University argue, "Some of our 'best people' may well feel called to live a celibate lifestyle in ministry. Others may not. But if some of our 'best people' who claim to hear a call to ministerial priesthood are denied . . . simply because . . . they choose to live a life of expressive love, a great injustice has been done to the people, and to the God who authored the call in the first place."

But others see celibacy as the most magnanimous act of self-giving that a priest can offer—a necessary gesture of ultimate devotion and service. "The church sees chastity as something very positive," explains Bishop George Lucas of Springfield, Illinois. "All are called to chastity. Some are called to committed celibacy. At its best, celibacy keeps us transparent. People can approach us, women and men, girls and boys, as if they were approaching Jesus himself. . . . If we practice [celibacy] in a healthy way, people will see through us to Jesus. In our ministry they will hear his voice and recognize his hospitality."

The debate about mandatory clerical celibacy will likely continue as church reformers and traditionalists continue to examine ways to address the priest shortage. This and other challenging questions are explored in the following chapters of *Opposing Viewpoints: The Catholic Church:* What Is the State of the Catholic Church? What Led to the Sex Abuse Scandal in the Catholic Church? Should the Catholic Church Try to Influence Politics and Culture? Should the Catholic Church Be Reformed? Contributors to this volume offer a unique investigation of the political, ethical, and theological controversies surrounding the Catholic Church.

CHAPTER 1

What Is the State of the Catholic Church?

Chapter Preface

The Roman Catholic Church is one of the most prominent religious institutions in the world. Claiming at least a billion members worldwide, it occupies an exceptional position as the sole religious organization with permanent observer status in the United Nations General Assembly. In the United States, the Catholic Church maintains a significant degree of political and social influence as the country's largest Christian denomination.

The American Catholic Church, however, has been confronted with a series of deeply disturbing revelations of child sexual abuse by its clergy. As the scandal unfolded in 2002, evidence emerged proving that the American church hierarchy knew of patterns of sexual abuse by some of its priests yet continued to allow these men access to children. The public drew the unavoidable conclusion that church authorities were at best ignorant of how to deal with child sexual abuse and at worst actively covering up the problem. Feeling stunned and betrayed, many among the American Catholic laity responded by demanding greater decision-making power in church governance and much more accountability from their bishops. The result has been a flowering of church-related activism among ordinary Catholics. As journalists Bret Schulte and Rochelle Sharpe note, a significant outcome of the sex abuse scandal is that "the American Catholic Church is no longer governed solely by all-powerful bishops. Sex-abuse victims, police investigators, prosecutors, and insurance companies have forced a new openness in the church and unbolted the door to lay Catholics clamoring to get involved."

This "new openness" in the American Catholic Church highlights a decades-old tension among two groups of practicing Catholics: those influenced by Vatican II, an early 1960s council that promoted modern reforms, and those who wish to maintain or restore elements of a pre-Vatican II church. "Vatican II Catholics" include moderates and liberals who challenge the church's traditional rejection of artificial birth control, married clergy, divorce, homosexuality, and ordainment of women. In light of the sex-abuse scandals, many Vatican II Catholics maintain that the church's archaic attitudes about sexuality created an atmosphere of clerical secrecy and repression that contributed to the pathology of child sexual abuse. Conservative Catholics, on the other hand, generally support the church's traditional teachings on sexuality, gender roles, worship, and clerical celibacy. These conservatives often argue that it is the liberalized attitudes promoted by Vatican II-influenced clergy that helped to spread the kind of immorality that culminated in child sexual abuse.

For some observers, these clashing attitudes concerning doctrine and the sex-abuse scandal suggest that the Roman Catholic Church is suffering from a case of "split personality," and that such deeply rooted divisions threaten to throw the church into a schism. Yet others argue that this discord is evidence of a vibrant, thriving community with enough breadth to embrace believers of widely ranging political and theological opinions. In the following chapter authors present diverse views on the state of the Catholic Church in the modern world, examining the legacy of Pope John Paul II, recent charges of Catholic anti-Semitism, and the role of various factions within the church.

"The very authority of the Church has been struck a blow."

The Sex Abuse Scandal Has Caused Lasting Damage to the Church

James K. Fitzpatrick

The recent scandals involving priests who sexually abused children have caused long-term damage to the Catholic Church, argues James K. Fitzpatrick in the following viewpoint. Even though the number of pedophile priests is very small, church authorities' neglect and mismanagement of the crisis will make it more difficult for Catholics to take basic church teachings seriously, Fitzpatrick contends. Many Catholics are therefore less likely to accept the church's traditional stance on moral issues such as abortion, extramarital sex, and artificial birth control, he maintains. Fitzpatrick writes a weekly column for the *Wanderer*, a conservative Catholic periodical.

As you read, consider the following questions:
1. Who are some of the people and groups that have been using the sex abuse scandals to defame the Catholic Church, in Fitzpatrick's opinion?
2. What good, if any, might come out of the sex abuse scandals, according to the author?
3. What perception do many ordinary Catholics now hold of their priests and bishops, according to Fitzpatrick?

I don't like to say this, but we must face the facts. The rash of sex abuse scandals involving Catholic priests is causing lasting damage to the Church. Whether it can be undone in our lifetime is questionable. I don't think I am the only one who has heard loyal and dutiful Catholics speculating about how imprudent it now seems for them to have once routinely permitted their children to go on class trips escorted by priests.

This is a sad state of affairs, one I never thought I would live to witness. If the hierarchy and members of the clergy do not like hearing these things, that is the price that must be paid for letting these scandalous activities go on.

Pedophile Priests Are Rare

I don't want to go overboard in my criticism. I believe the number of pedophile priests to be very small. I attended Catholic schools from first grade through graduate school, and I never—not once—came across even credible rumors about the priests and brothers who were my teachers. One of my former colleagues at a public school where I taught was an ex-priest who left the priesthood and married without going through any of the procedures required by the Church. He didn't care in the least what the Church said about his decision, or anything else, for that matter.

This man harbored an undisguised contempt for the institutional Church. He would not hesitate for a second to use any information he possessed about pedophile priests to bash the hierarchy. But, in the many years I knew him, he never did, insisting that in all his time as a seminarian and priest in the Archdiocese of New York, he never encountered homosexual behavior. And, I repeat, this man would tell tales if he had any to tell. He never hesitated to criticize priests and bishops for what he perceived to be other vices: excessive drinking, mean-spiritedness, anti-intellectualism, shallowness, and hypocrisy, for example.

Let us also state the obvious. There are those who are using these stories about pedophile priests to defame the Church, including people and groups that have spent the last 25 years defending the homosexual revolution. But even a broken clock is right twice a day. It is hard to defend Boston's [former] Cardinal Law, regardless of the sleazy nature of some of his accusers. It is now clear that he transferred priests accused of abusing children from parish to parish, rather than reporting their criminal behavior to the proper authorities. Protecting the Church's reputation is important, but not that important.

The Double Standard

If any good can come out of these sad days for the Church, it may be that those in authority in the Church will become more vigilant in their duties from now on. But even if that happens, the damage has been done. And I do not mean just the increased sexual suspicion that the ordinary Catholic will feel from now on about their priests and members of religious orders. The very authority of the Church has been struck a blow. You don't have to be a rocket scientist to spot the double standard.

Margulies. © 2002 by the *New Jersey Record*. Reproduced by permission.

People will take note of how Church authorities covered up for pedophile priests, while at the same time denying annulments to devout practicing Catholics and refusing the sacraments to divorced Catholics and those who have had abortions. One wonders how engaged couples will accept being scolded for "living in sin," considering what they have seen in these sex scandals. The folks in the pews will see that the rules are not always the rules.

This time we are not talking about Church authorities changing the rules about eating meat on Friday and the Latin Mass. We are talking about exceptions to the rules for priests who sexually abused young boys, who committed a crime. You can be sure that Catholics will remember, the next time they are told it is their obligation to accept the hard teachings of the Church governing their personal behavior. Why accept the Church's teachings on abortion, extramarital sex, and birth control, when the clerics who demand obedience in these matters become trimmers when they or their friends behave immorally?

Undoing the Damage

Please do not misread me. I am not saying that these cover-ups for pedophile priests somehow invalidate the Church's teachings. That would be silly. Thinking Catholics know that. But not every Catholic takes the time to ponder the difference between the teachings of the Church and those in authority who propound them, between the message and the messenger. The issue at hand is perception, and perception is reality. The perception among a good number of ordinary Catholics will be that, while priests and bishops talk tough about our obligations to accept the teachings of the Church, they do not live up to them in their own lives. That will make a difference.

We were once told "once a priest, always a priest," but discovered that this is not quite the case, that a priest can be laicized.[1] We were told that "a marriage is forever," and then read in our newspapers of wealthy Catholic politicians and entertainers being given annulments on highly questionable grounds. And now, even though the Bible tells us that "whoever causes one of these little ones who believe in me to sin, it would be better for him to have a great millstone fastened

---

1. Laicization is the process that legally returns a priest or other cleric to the status of a layperson.

around his neck and to be drowned in the depth of the sea"
—that there are exceptions to be made for members of the clergy. Their punishment is being assigned to a new parish.

Obviously, not all of the members of the hierarchy were as negligent in this matter as those in Massachusetts. But all of the hierarchy—and the good and faithful clergy in general—now have the responsibility of undoing this damage. They have no choice. It may very well be the work of their lifetimes.

| *"Hierarchies come and go; the faith endures."*

The Sex Abuse Scandal Has Not Caused Lasting Damage to the Church

Richard P. McBrien

The recent scandal over clerical sexual abuse of children constitutes a serious crisis for the Catholic Church, but it has not undermined Catholic faith, contends Richard P. McBrien in the following viewpoint. While Catholics may lose confidence in the church's hierarchy and in some priests, they can still treasure the sacraments and place their trust in God, the author concludes. McBrien is a priest, essayist, and professor of theology at the University of Notre Dame.

As you read, consider the following questions:

1. Why is the sex abuse scandal the most serious crisis for the modern Catholic Church, in McBrien's opinion?
2. According to the author, why do Catholics remain in the church?
3. Why, in McBrien's view, is the sex abuse crisis not a crisis of faith?

Richard P. McBrien, "Crisis Threatens Sacraments, but Not Faith; Despite Blow to Priesthood, Bishops' Actions Do Not Undermine Catholic Truth," *National Catholic Reporter*, vol. 8, June 21, 2002, pp. 20–21. Copyright © 2002 by the *National Catholic Reporter*. Reproduced by permission of the author.

The sex abuse crisis that has been at the center of our attention these past few months may be the most serious crisis the Roman Catholic church has faced in modern times, but it does not involve a crisis of faith.

First, why is the crisis so serious? Because Catholicism is, in its very essence, a sacramental faith and a sacramental community, and the priesthood is essential to its sacramental life. This crisis points a dagger at the heart of the priesthood, raising questions about its integrity, its spiritual health and its viability.

Why Catholics Remain in the Church

Catholics remain in the church not because of the pope or the bishops, but because they wish to continue drawing upon the spiritual riches of its sacramental life. They celebrate the birth of a new daughter or son, or a new grandchild, in the sacrament of baptism, a celebration that is not limited to the formal rite in which water is poured on the infant's forehead while the priest recites the words, "I baptize you in the name of the Father, and of the Son, and of the Holy Spirit." Rather, it involves the whole baptismal event: the preparations, the gathering at the baptismal font, the reception and gift giving.

Catholics celebrate a loved one's coming of age with the sacrament of confirmation, and their embarking on a whole new stage of life in the sacrament of matrimony.

They gather around a loved one who is seriously ill, expressing their solidarity and support in the sacrament of the anointing of the sick. Like baptism, that sacrament is not limited to the rite of anointing alone. It involves the whole process of caring for the sick person, of praying together, of aiding in the loved one's recovery, if that be God's will.

And should the loved one die, the ritual includes the wake, the funeral liturgy, the burial, and the subsequent gathering for a meal and visitation. It is also an occasion for celebration of, and thanksgiving for, the life of the deceased.

Catholics seek the consolation of the sacrament of reconciliation (also known as penance or simply confession) when they fall from the standard of the gospel. While relatively few Catholics take advantage of the auricular form of the sacrament today (confessing sins directly to the priest in a confessional or reconciliation room), they flock to church whenever a communal penance service is held.

Churches Are Still Crowded

There's no question that this sex-abuse scandal has changed the landscape, changed the whole situation. After this scandal the whole question of credibility in the church, respectability of the clerical, episcopal authority in the church, looms large. A good number of people in the hierarchy have been tainted with this scandal, and that has shaken the faith and confidence of a lot of people. . . .

[But] one thing that amazes me is that churches are still crowded. People are going to church. Attendance is down to be sure, but people are going. People want to practice their religion, so they weave their way through this conflict. . . .

[In my] parish we worship together, we try to live a good life. We try to help the poor, feed the hungry, have a prison ministry. We do all the corporal works of mercy, and we're very engaged and very involved. . . .

Why do I go to church on Sunday? I go to church because I want to pray. I want to celebrate the Eucharist. But I also go to church to remind me that I belong to a community, a community that cares about other people. I don't get that inspiration from the late-night news or the *Chicago Tribune*. I get that inspiration from my church, from my religion.

Jay P. Dolan, *U.S. Catholic*, October 2003.

They also have a real, though incomplete, experience of the sacrament at the beginning of each Eucharist when the presider calls upon the congregation to be mindful of its sins and to ask God's forgiveness.

The Eucharist

But at the heart and center of the church's sacramental life is the Eucharist itself, which the Second Vatican Council called the summit and the source of the whole Christian life.[1] It is

1. The Eucharist, or "Holy Communion," is the sacrament in which bread and wine is consecrated by a priest and shared as the body and blood of Jesus Christ. The Second Vatican Council was a series of meetings and discussions among bishops that resulted in various modern reforms to the church. This council convened between 1962 and 1965.

at the Eucharist that the church becomes most visibly present and active in the world. It is the Body of Christ, the Temple of the Holy Spirit, and the People of God at worship, participating sacramentally in Christ's worship of the Father, in and through the power of the Holy Spirit.

And presiding over that central act of worship is one who has been commissioned to that high pastoral and ministerial responsibility by the sacrament of holy orders.

Without the sacrament of holy orders, there is no Eucharist. And without an adequate number of psychologically and spiritually healthy priests, the church is, to a large degree, deprived of the gift of the Eucharist.

Once again, it is because of the sacraments that Catholics remain in, and draw spiritual nourishment from, the mystery of the church. After Jesus Christ himself, the Holy Spirit, and the gospel, the sacraments are the Catholic church's greatest assets.

Not a Crisis of Faith

Why, then, is this crisis not also a crisis of faith? Because the failures of individual priests and their bishops do not challenge, much less undermine, the truth that defines and distinguishes Catholicism.

This is a major crisis, to be sure, but it is a crisis of confidence and trust in the bishops as a group and in some of the church's priests as well. It is not a crisis of faith.

We can still believe in the God who created us, who sustains us and who promises us eternal life.

We can still believe in the Christ who redeemed us and who offers himself as a model of human life itself. And we can still believe in the Holy Spirit who makes all things new and who is the power by which we hope to be fully transformed in the end.

Hierarchies come and go; the faith endures.

*"He was a great pope. He was close to people
of all races. He was close to the poor and
rich, and he taught the young how to
breathe their faith."*

The Papacy of John Paul II Was a Success

Jeffrey Fleishman

Born Karol Wojtyla, Pope John Paul II (1920–2005) had a profound effect on non-Catholics as well as Catholics, reports Jeffrey Fleishman in the following viewpoint. At his funeral mass on April 8, 2005, which drew a crowd of 4 million pilgrims, people of various backgrounds remembered John Paul II as a dedicated and devout leader who championed human rights, peace, and morality. Observers note that John Paul II was especially beloved by the young, who admired his concern for all people and his respect for transcendental truths. Fleishman is a staff writer for the *Los Angeles Times*.

As you read, consider the following questions:

1. What made the funeral of John Paul II "an evocative moment in history," according to Fleishman?
2. According to the author, why was Nepalese student Samman Khatewoda attending the funeral of John Paul II?
3. How many world dignitaries attended John Paul II's funeral, according to Fleishman?

The crowds gathered before first light Friday [April 8, 2005], swelling over bridges and through narrow streets, surging toward St. Peter's Square, where nuns knelt and boys straddled the shoulders of fathers to glimpse Pope John Paul II's coffin move through a morning of broken clouds.

Hundreds of thousands clapped and chanted, "Giovanni Paolo, Giovanni Paolo." The roar rippled like a wave and then quieted. Bibles opened to the soft notes of an organ. The young and dreadlocked, the old and stooped stood side by side in a tide of humanity that was at once spectacle, faithful devotion and an evocative moment in history.

"The World's Father"

The crowds for the funeral Mass—estimated at 4 million— were giddy and tearful, joyous and reverent. They mourned a spiritual leader but celebrated his long and rich life. Teen-agers fiddled with cameras and cellphones. Young priests sobbed. Silver-haired ladies said the rosary.

And Poles, tens of thousands of them, prayed with pride after traveling more than a thousand miles in cramped trains and cars for a last glance at their native son.

"He was our father," said Wojciech Piegza, who had a Pol-ish flag wrapped around his neck. "He was the world's father."

Pilgrims flowed out of St. Peter's and down Via della Con-ciliazione toward Castel Sant' Angelo. Thousands poured in from side streets to watch the Mass on towering television screens. Police manned metal barricades, helicopters thrummed overhead, and emergency workers, glowing in neon green and orange clothing, flickered past centuries-old statues of saints and angels.

"I'm not a Catholic. I'm from Nepal," said Samman Khate-woda, a university student majoring in fine arts. "I came here out of respect for the Catholic religion. John Paul was a good man. I think millions of people must be here. The president of the United States is here. I think right now we are at the center of the world."

Many pilgrims recounted the days when John Paul, the most widely traveled pontiff in history, landed in their coun-try aboard his plane, Shepherd One.

"I was in Lourdes [France] for his visit and in Paris for

World Youth Day," said Clemence Giral, who had traveled from France. "I'm happy to be here and confident that John Paul II is with God. He did a lot of good with his prayers. . . . Thanks to him, now we know the way to paradise. The spirit of John Paul II will illuminate the new pope."

Daniela Puddu remembered when she stood in St. Peter's more than 26 years ago as a child.

The Suffering Servant

In life, no other great figure in the second half of the 20th century seemed to inhabit his role so utterly, yet in so many different ways. There was the itinerant evangelist with the lit-from-within smile, conducting his never-ending crusade. There was the mystic who, as an observer noted, "made decisions on his knees."

There was the subtle geopolitician who refuted Stalin's famous sneer "How many divisions has the Pope?" at the expense of the dictator's heirs. The moral philosopher who lectured at Harvard.

And finally, the suffering servant. "He was a thoroughly, radically committed Christian disciple who really believed, as he put it, that 'Jesus Christ is the answer to the question that is every human life,'" says George Weigel, a biographer of the Pope. "The rest followed from that.". . .

In his evangelization, he was so terribly urgent; in his doctrine, so unbending; for the children, so utterly hopeful. He was unconscious of self. He was so full of energy and reluctant to acknowledge when he was spent. He was so Christlike in his sense of fate. . . . He was so dedicated to his mission, so certain that this was God's plan and himself a part of it.

David Van Biema, CNN.com, April 12, 2005.

"I was in the square when John Paul was elected pope," she said. "I was 11 years old and he stayed in my life like a relative. He was a great pope. He was close to people of all races. He was close to poor and rich, and he taught the young how to breathe their faith."

Rita Mauro drove up from Calabria in southern Italy. "Coming here is something we did for the pope," she said. "We've been here since Wednesday afternoon and have attended everything. It's nice to be here. This has been a sweet and soft experience. I am surprised by the participation of the people. I always was touched by the pope, but the fact that he was loved by so many young people was a revelation to me."

Winds stiffened and flags from Poland, Spain, France and Bosnia-Herzegovina snapped amid choral hymns. The ground was covered with sleeping bags, water bottles and clumps of backpacks. Pilgrims, many bleary-eyed and scraggly from spending a night in the cold, huddled under blankets. A few leaned on lampposts and slept. A man lifted a large cutout of a golden heart, which glimmered in the sunshine until the sky turned the color of slate.

Two hundred dignitaries, including President [George W.] Bush and Italian Prime Minister Silvio Berlusconi, were specks in a sea of bishops and cardinals to most mourners, who pushed and strained and finally resigned themselves that they could get no closer to the pope's wooden coffin at the steps of the basilica.

"The pope showed us faith in getting our Poland back from the communists," said Marcin Janecki, who borrowed money from a stranger to travel 24 hours on a train from Katowice in southern Poland. "I was a young boy at the beginning of his papacy. My parents taught me about him. He was a great man. He took on poverty and war and peace and morality.

"He made us focus on problems we don't want to because we think too much of making money or getting ahead. He showed us transcendence."

The media universe, the realm the pope so often courted, moved through the crowds and camped at their edge. Images flashed across screens, loudspeakers roared. Thousands of pilgrims held digital cameras, recording the flesh and blood before their eyes. It was this magnetic power that John Paul understood, and it seemed fitting that his funeral would be as electronic for many as it was redemptive for others.

The Mass ended. The cardinals disappeared into the basilica. The heads of state gathered their entourages. The pallbearers lifted John Paul's coffin.

Another wave rolled through the crowd: "Giovanni Paolo, Giovanni Paolo." It was over, but no one was quite sure what to do. There was stillness, a few more tears and then the shuffle of feet over blackened cobblestones toward train stations and highways leading home in the rain.

"If you judge a successful leader by the caliber of men he inspires to follow him, then the judgment on John Paul II is damning."

The Papacy of John Paul II Was Deeply Flawed

Andrew Sullivan

The papacy of John Paul II, who served as leader of the Catholic Church from 1978 to 2005, was a deep disappointment, writes Andrew Sullivan in the following viewpoint. According to Sullivan, John Paul II used his acting skills and media savvy to reassert the church's authority in a counterproductive way. To suppress many of the modern changes instituted by the Second Vatican Council of the early 1960s, John Paul II silenced debate about priestly celibacy, women in the priesthood, and homosexuality. In addition, Sullivan notes, the child sexual abuse scandal and the decline in the numbers and the quality of Catholic priests occurred during the papacy of John Paul II. Sullivan is a senior editor of the *New Republic*, a weekly magazine.

As you read, consider the following questions:

1. Why does Sullivan see John Paul II as an "idiosyncratic" intellectual?
2. How did John Paul II influence Catholic teaching on "culture of life" issues, according to the author?
3. What was John Paul II deeply afraid of, in Sullivan's opinion?

Andrew Sullivan, "Washington Diarist: Superstar," *The New Republic*, April 18, 2005, p. 46. Copyright © 2005 by The New Republic, Inc. Reproduced by permission.

He was an actor. And his greatest and most innovative skill as pontiff was the creation of drama and symbolism. You only had to observe one of his peripatetic papal visits to see that, as I was lucky enough to do in San Antonio. The modern-looking stage, the vast crowds that this Pope knew he could summon anywhere in the world, the carefully planned photo-ops—they all created a series of mirrors focusing back on the man himself. He communicated as much by stirring addresses in dozens of languages as by a deeply creased brow, a smile, or a tear. This dramatization of self continued until his death. We have been told that his last gesture was an attempt to bless the huge crowd assembled outside St Peter's. He was on stage until the end.

Before him, none of this was imaginable. Karol Wojtyla took the painstakingly acquired, centuries-long mystique of the secluded, scared papacy and cashed it in across the globe. His superstar presence alone was the overwhelming message—whether to those in Africa who felt excluded from the global church; or to the Poles chafing under Soviet tyranny; or to those Catholics in Central and South America battling poverty, inequality, and the growing force of evangelical Protestantism. Even English Catholics felt something profound when the Pope visited Great Britain for the first time since the Reformation. The Church had always understood the importance of pageantry and drama and personality. But Wojtyla actually reinvented the form for a world of mass media.

Silencing Dissent

It took a while to realize that this personalization of the Church—and its identification with one man before all others—was more than drama. Wojtyla leveraged this new stardom to reassert a far older idea of the papacy—as the central, unaccountable force in the Church. The Second Vatican Council [of the early 1960s] had opened authority up, placing the hierarchy on a more equal footing with the lay faithful in understanding the tenets of faith. It had also led to all sorts of chaotic improvisation and confusion. Wojtyla shut this process down—the good alongside the bad. He didn't reverse the Council (it was beyond his will or power). But he ignored and suppressed it in critical areas. National churches were given little leeway. Dissent within the Church was forbidden. The Pope silenced even debate of issues that were not of fundamental doctrinal importance, such as the prudential, managerial questions of whether priests could marry or whether women could become priests. These, he asserted, were eternal arrangements that were beyond discussion, even if maintaining them had led to a crisis in the Church's very existence in some countries.

Unfulfilled Expectations

After Vatican II [the council that engaged in an influential reform process between 1962 and 1965] many Catholics believed that the papacy would be less monarchical. . . . John Paul II disappointed this expectation. The Church in his pontificate has become more centralized, not less so. The appointment of bishops has been tightly controlled. In Austria, Switzerland, Brazil, and elsewhere, "unpopular" bishops have been appointed. Right-wing movements like Opus Dei and Communion and Liberation (*Communione e Liberazione*) have been encouraged. . . .

John Paul believed [the Church] was undergoing a crisis of identity. . . . The remedy was to stress those things that divided Catholics from other Christians—papal infallibility, Mariology [theology focusing on the role of the Virgin Mary], defense of Paul VI's encyclical on birth control (*Humanae Vitae*), and the presentation of homosexuality as a "disorder." Priestly identity was also reasserted: the Catholic priest was to be celibate for life, dressed in clericals, spiritual, and "above" or at any rate "out of" politics. Nuns were to resume wearing their habits. Theologians were to be docile and not raise awkward questions.

Peter Hebblethwaite, *HarperCollins Encyclopedia of Catholicism*, 1995.

This man so hostile to intellectual debate was, paradoxically, an intellectual, although an idiosyncratic one. His faith was a strange mixture of esoteric phenomenological reflections and medieval attachments to various saints, miracles, and practices. He made few fundamental changes. But he resolutely appointed loyalists to every position he could, and he elevated the secretive and ultra-conservative order of Opus Dei to unheard-of influence. On matters of human sexuality and the "culture of life," he moved Catholic teaching away from prudential balance to eternal absolutes—that life is equally sacred, whether it is a nanosecond after conception or decades into a persistent vegetative state. The distinctions made by Catholics in the past—between, say, a naturally aborted embryo and a third-trimester baby, or between "ordinary" and "extraordinary" means for maintaining life—were downplayed. Why? Perhaps because the Pope believed the danger of new technologies required as radical an opposition as possible.

A Collapsing Church

Did he succeed? If, by success, we mean the maintenance of the truth in the face of error, then only God knows. If, by success, we mean asserting the truths of Christianity against the lies of communism, then the answer is an unequivocal yes. But if, by success, we mean winning the argument against secular democracy in the West, the answer must be no. This European Pope oversaw an unprecedented collapse of the Church in its European heartland. Under his papacy, vocations for the priesthood barely kept up with population in the developing world and simply collapsed in the West. Protestantism boomed in South America. Mass attendance in North America fell, along with donations. And the quality of the priesthood went from mediocre to terrible. If you judge a successful leader by the caliber of men he inspires to follow him, then the judgment on John Paul II is damning.

Under his papacy, the Church was also guilty of allowing the rape and molestation of vast numbers of children and teenagers, and of systematically covering the crimes up. It is hard to understand how the leader of any lay organization would have stayed in office after allowing such criminality. But how the leader of the Catholic Church survived without even an attempt at papal accountability is still astonishing. A Pope who devoted enormous energy to explicating why the only moral expression of human sexuality is marital heterosexual intercourse presided over the rape of thousands of children by his own priests. What was his response? He protected the chief enabler of the abuse in the United States, Cardinal Bernard Law, and used the occasion of his own Church's failing to blame homosexuals in general. Attempting to grapple with the real question would have meant a debate about priestly celibacy, homosexuality, pedophilia, and the Church's disproportionately gay priesthood. But this Pope was far more interested in closing debates than in opening them.

I have a personal stake in this as well, of course. I'm a Catholic now withdrawn from Communion whose entire adult life has been in Wojtyla's shadow. And, as a homosexual, I watched as the Church refused to grapple with even basic questions and ran, terrified, from its own deep psychosexual dysfunction. "Be not afraid," this Pope counseled us. But he was deeply afraid of the complicated truth about human sexuality and the dark truth about his own Church's crimes. This was a Pope who, above all, knew how to look away. . . . But people—faithful people—noticed where he couldn't look. And they grieved, even as, in the aftermath of this brittle, showboating papacy, they now hope.

*"Anti-Semitic hatred and enmity was
embedded in the doctrine, theology,
and liturgy of the Catholic Church."*

The Catholic Church Has Not Acknowledged Its Anti-Semitism

Daniel Jonah Goldhagen

Daniel Jonah Goldhagen is a political scientist at Harvard University and the author of *A Moral Reckoning: The Role of the Catholic Church in the Holocaust and Its Unfulfilled Duty of Repair*, from which this viewpoint is excerpted. Goldhagen argues that the Catholic Church bears moral blame for the Jewish Holocaust during World War II. For one thing, Catholic doctrine taught that all Jews were responsible for the death of Jesus Christ, a teaching that fueled the anti-Semitism of the time. In addition, Catholic clergy noticeably refused to denounce the human rights violations that culminated in mass executions of Jews—implying an acceptance of such atrocities. The church's failure to acknowledge and redress this anti-Semitism is a betrayal of Jews and Catholics alike, Goldhagen concludes.

As you read, consider the following questions:

1. In Goldhagen's opinion, what is the most injurious anti-Semitic charge that has ever been expressed?
2. When can silence about public actions be construed as approval of them, in the author's view?
3. Why does the Catholic Church's attempt to help some Jews appear halfhearted, according to Goldhagen?

Anti-Semitism, and this is true of other kinds of prejudice, is baseless antipathy or animus, which in itself constitutes unjust discrimination. In the [Catholic] Church's terms, it is a violation of the Eighth Commandment, "You shall not bear false witness against your neighbor," which, according to Church doctrine, mandates that *respect for the reputation* of persons forbids every attitude and word likely to cause them unjust injury." When Jews live in a profoundly anti-Semitic culture, they live in a culture of hostility, a culture that not only inevitably leads to further unjust discriminatory acts but is itself, by definition, harmfully discriminatory. It is discriminatory and injurious because a Jew, a Jewish child, is disliked, thought ill of, hated, before the anti-Semites know anything else about her as an individual, and for alleged attributes that are not, and will never be, hers. The anti-Semites think ill of her only because of her identity as a Jew. Feeling antipathy or animus toward a person for such a reason is to perpetrate an injustice, which is to inflict harm. The Catholic Church agrees. . . .

Anti-semitism, a culture of hatred, coursed through the politics and societies of Europe during the 1930s and 1940s and through the corridors of the Church, from St. Peter's to the most humble parish chapel. It was an unremarkable feature of European Catholics' outlook, derived from the Christian Bible and from Church teachings. In many European countries it was well nigh impossible, especially for Catholic clergy, not to be exposed to anti-Semitism. The clergy knew that it was central to the political cultures of much of Europe, that it was being spread by politicians, secular and Church alike. All those who supported the offense of anti-Semitism, in this instance the offense being the political transgression of teaching and spreading it, bear moral blame for their approving stance. Given that anti-Semitism was the common sense of the institutional culture of the Catholic Church during this period—indeed it was at the time hard to be a Catholic priest and not to be anti-Semitic, since among the many other commonly held anti-Semitic charges, it was a central Catholic doctrine, based in Scripture, that contemporary Jews were guilty for the death of Jesus—it is safe to say that support for this offense and its attendant moral blame applies to the vast majority of clergy of these years, even if the character and intensity of their anti-Semitism varied widely.

Political Transgressions

For many of the Catholic bishops and priests who supported tyranny and anti-Semitism, their moral blame is mirrored by political blame for their political activities on behalf of the cause of tyranny and for spreading anti-Semitism. No one bears a greater burden of this kind than the two Popes, Pius XI and Pius XII (as Vatican Secretary of State), in their welcoming of the Nazis to power, which ushered in the destruction of the democratic institutions that they generally despised. Their Concordat lent early political legitimacy to the Hitler-led Nazi regime.[1] . . .

The political blame incurred by the Popes is shared by the German Church's clergy, who, exceptions notwithstanding, helped to legitimize Nazism. This is generally true also for Catholicism's national churches in Italy, France, Slovakia, Austria, and Croatia for their support of their own countries' criminal regimes.

It would be hard to exaggerate the extent of the Church's political blame for the political transgression of teaching millions of people libelous notions about Jews and therefore to feel animus and enmity toward them. The Vatican, national churches across Europe—in Germany, Poland, France, Italy, and elsewhere—published in their newspapers and periodicals the most damaging anti-Semitic libels, including especially identifying Jews with the Bolshevik [communist] threat. . . .

Catholic Anti-Semitism

Teaching Catholics that all Jews are guilty for crucifying Jesus, which was perhaps the most injurious anti-Semitic charge ever put forward, was official Catholic Church policy. Anti-Semitic hatred and enmity was embedded in the doctrine, theology, and liturgy of the Catholic Church,

---

1. In 1933 Pope Pius XI and Pius XII (then a cardinal) signed a Concordat, or treaty of cooperation, with Nazi Germany.

doled out in larger and smaller doses to Catholics . . . around Europe on a yearly, weekly, and daily basis. . . .

It is an absurdity to maintain that the Nazis would have invented their anti-Semitism out of thin air, or that their tens of millions of eager anti-Semitic followers would have thrown their lot in with the Nazis' dehumanizing and violent policies that followed on this wild, phantasmagoric prejudice, had the Catholic Church not already poisoned much of German and European culture with anti-Semitism. Cardinal Edward Cassidy, head of the Holy See's Commission for Religious Relations with the Jews, when addressing Jewish leaders in Washington in 1998, was not uninformed when he pointed a finger at the Catholic Church, declaring that "the ghetto, which came into being in 1555 with a papal bull, became in Nazi Germany the antechamber of the extermination." It would also be absurd to think that the Church's sustained propagation of anti-Semitism during the Nazi period did not reinforce popular support around Europe for the eliminationist persecution of the Jews. Had the two Popes, the Church leaders and lower clergy used their pulpits and their enormous number of newspapers and diocesan publications with their huge, faithful readerships in Germany and around Europe to declare anti-Semitism a vicious delusion and to denounce the persecution of the Jews as a grievous crime and sin, then the political history of Europe would have been different, and the fate of the Jews much better.

But this did not happen. Pius XI and Pius XII were anti-Semites. They were prone, as they themselves gave evidence —Pius XI with his reports from Poland of 1918 and Pius XII with his report of 1919 on the Communist insurrection in Munich—to almost Nazi-like fantasies and libels about Jews. Their supervision, approval, and tolerance of . . . Church publications spreading the most incendiary kind of anti-Semitic libels and accusations continued steadily during the Nazi period. Catholic bishops and priests in Germany and across Europe were also anti-Semites. . . .

Incurring Moral Guilt

The moral guilt that accrues to people for supporting crime was extremely widespread within the Church although it varied substantially depending on the given crime. The Church as a whole and bishops and priests across Europe supported the anti-Jewish laws passed in Germany and then in similar form in Italy, Vichy,[2] Slovakia, Croatia, and other countries. How could they not, when the laws merely codified what many organs of the Church had themselves been urging, and of which the Church officially approved? These laws, containing scores of provisions that gravely violated the Jews' human rights, were clearly criminal. The understanding and support for such laws was especially substantial in the German Catholic Church, where the belief in the Jews' putative criminal nature and the alleged great danger they posed was strong.

To be more specific, the Germans (and their helpers abroad) subjected Jews to a range of criminal policies. Before the war these anti-Jewish policies included legal and administrative measures that forbade Jews from holding government jobs, especially in the civil service, and from practicing their professions and participating in the economy; that isolated Jews from non-Jews by excluding them from using public facilities, including schools and swimming pools; that turned them into political and social pariahs by stripping them of their citizenship and prohibiting them from marrying or having sexual relations with non-Jews; that drove them to emigrate; and that subjected them to violence including physical assault, incarceration in concentration camps, burning of their synagogues and communal buildings, and episodic murder.

During the war the Germans augmented these policies with a set of new ones: forced deportation, ghettoization, murder through starvation, debilitation, and disease (even prior to the formal program of total annihilation), a greatly expanded and ever more brutal camp system, enslavement, and systematic, comprehensive mass murder. All of these policies furthered the Germans' two central objectives: producing the "social death" of Jews (turning them into violently dominated, natally alienated, and generally dishonored beings, against whom one might do anything) and eliminating

2. Vichy is a reference to Nazi-occupied France between 1940 and 1944.

the Jews and their "influence" wherever Germany ruled, eventually with the essentially open policy of extermination.

These policies were at the heartless core of Germany's politics during the 1930s and 1940s. Knowledge of them, indeed contact with them, was all but unavoidable. The German bishops and priests knew them all well (as did the Vatican and clergy across Europe). How did they view them? There is no evidence that even a significant minority of them viewed the two central German anti-Jewish policy objectives of these years with disapproval. These interrelated criminal aims—making the Jews socially dead and eliminating their influence and contact with Germans—were based on an image of Jewish infiltration and danger that accorded with what the Church had been preaching all along. Individual churchmen sometimes disapproved of individual aspects of this eliminationist assault. Some looked upon the violence with distaste and some with disapproval and horror, but we have little evidence even of this or that the disapproval was a heartfelt, deep strain within the German Catholic Church. In fact, the evidence of the German Church's acceptance and approval of Germany's criminal eliminationist program, short of the murderous violence, is overwhelming. The compatibility of the Nazi regime's and the German Catholic Church's aspirations in this matter is striking. Even after *Kristallnacht*, the German Catholic Church, its bishops and priests, were silent.[3] . . .

Only mass murder may have failed to find overwhelming understanding within the German Church hierarchy. Yet the evidence of widespread principled, unequivocal moral condemnation among the German clergy even of their countrymen's slaughter of the Jews is also not substantial. . . .

A Thundering Silence

The silence of German priests in the apocalyptic killing fields of the east—when they were not actively lending approval with their words—was reproduced by Catholic clergy across Europe. During the Nazi period the Church emanated a

---

3. Kristallnacht, the "Night of Broken Glass," was a massive anti-Semitic pogrom that occurred in Germany on November 9, 1938, during which the windows of Jewish-owned shops were broken.

great deal of silence. Silence is a critical issue here. It has two aspects. Silence constitutes a decision not to act against something, an act of omission. . . . It may also be an affirmative act indicating support for the uncommented-upon deed. In the face of great evil, silence from those who are publicly deemed morally responsible for speaking out can reasonably be construed as approval.

The Church's Failure

The Church's failure to denounce publicly or privately early Nazi violence aimed at Jews, a failure rooted in the Church's own anti-Semitism and its own theology, was part of what allowed that violence to become genocidal. Crucial to its building to a point of no return was Hitler's discovery (late) of the political indifference of the democracies to the fate of the Jews, and his discovery (early) of the moral and religious indifference of Christians to that fate. Nothing laid bare such indifference more dramatically than the Nazi-Vatican concordat and the *Reichstheologie* of the German Catholic Church—both of which sought the restoration of a civilization that excluded Jews. The steps from "Jews out!" to "Jews dead!," from religious elimination to physical elimination— from elimination, that is, to extermination—would prove all too small.

James Carroll, *Constantine's Sword: The Church and the Jews*, 2001.

The Church, its national churches, individual bishops and priests were virtually professional critics of things they deemed to violate the moral law. After all, their vocational duty, in the words of Pius XII's inaugural encyclical of 1939, was "to testify to the truth with Apostolic Firmness." Their self-understood calling, therefore, was to bring to the attention of their parishioners and of communal and political authorities matters that threatened the physical or moral well-being of their flock. The Church and its clergy habitually rendered judgment, criticism, condemnation of aspects of politics or society of which they disapproved. Even a cursory look at Popes' pronouncements, bishops' statements, and priests' sermons and at Church publications, its journals and newspapers, reveals a highly outspoken, interventionist institution and staff, both before and during World War II. Yet with regard to the brutal eliminationist persecution of the Jews, overwhelmingly there was silence. The Church, when it was not expressing its explicit approval of one or another aspect of the persecution, thundered silence. . . .

Let me be clear. I am not saying that the Pope and the clergy in general actively wanted the Jews to die. But aside from the small percentage of clergy who aided the Jews, we cannot be sure that the Catholic clergy in general opposed the mass annihilation. We cannot be sure that if they did, then they opposed it unequivocally and with all their hearts. We cannot be sure that they beheld the killing of the Jews, whom many of them deemed guilty of the gravest offenses, unambiguously as a crime and a sin. And we have such doubts because of the widespread anti-Semitism among them and because of the things that many of them did. We can be sure that a significant number of bishops and priests willingly contributed to the annihilation of the Jews. We can also be sure that the Pope's and the clergy's stunning lack of public sympathy for the Jews, their aid for critical acts of criminality, their support for so many more, and their extensive political blame and guilt definitively implicate the Catholic Church broadly and deeply in the crimes of the Germans, Croats, Lithuanians, Slovaks, and others against the Jews.

Occasional Attempts to Help Jews

The Catholic churchmen's multiple offenses and considerable culpability notwithstanding, we should bear in mind that the Church and its officials occasionally did try to help Jews, and some also did feel qualms or more over the eliminationist violence, especially the mass murder.

The Catholic Church, Pius XII, and the leadership of a few national churches made occasional attempts to help Jews. They were not particularly vigorous or sustained attempts, and they tended to come late in the war, after the Germans had already killed most of the Jews of a given country, and when the Allies were clearly going to win the war. When defending the Jews mattered a great deal, before the killing operations began or while they were just getting going, the Church watched silently. When it might have done the most good, namely, during the 1930s at the initial stages of the Germans' violent eliminationist persecution, when the Jews' persecutors passed dehumanizing race laws and robbed them of their livelihoods, professions, and homes, the Catholic Church, across Europe, was an antagonist of the Jews. And the most significant possible interventions—thunderous public condemnation by Pius XI or Pius XII, excommunication of all those persecuting Jews, an explicit call to all Europeans to help Jews—never came at all. This unwillingness to help Jews stands in the starkest contrast to the Church's regular interventions on behalf of Catholics who had converted from Judaism or of Jews covered by the sacrament of marriage to Catholics. For their welfare, the Church was genuinely concerned, and it intervened for them immediately, vigorously, and with evident passion. The Church's rare, weak, and late interventions on behalf of just some Jews have the unmistakable earmarks of halfhearted moves by people wanting to cover their backs for the coming postwar world. . . .

Forsaking Catholics' Souls

The act that may be, in a certain sense, the Church's greatest offense has not been even mentioned: its failure to Catholics. . . . ·

The Church did not tell Catholics that with every anti-Semitic act of omission or of participation—most obviously by actively participating, in any way, in the mass annihilation of the Jews—they committed a crime against humanity and a sin against God. The Church thereby allowed Catholics to place their souls at risk for an eternity in hell. According to the Church, the failure to have warned Catholics is a sin because we incur the "responsibility for the sins committed by others" by "not disclosing them when we have an obligation to do so." With this offense (and this is, of course, also true of the failure to warn Jews), the Catholic Church, its national churches, two popes, its bishops and priests offended God and failed Catholics as badly as a religious leader can fail those who look to him for guidance.

The Church, Pius XII, and the clergy (some of this applies also to Pius XI) allowed Catholics to persecute and perpetrate unjust harm upon Jews for one of two reasons: because the churchmen did not conceive of the anti-Jewish onslaught, including the mass killing, as crimes; or because they thought the various components of the German-led violent eliminationist persecution were crimes and, with their silence, chose to allow (act of omission) Catholics to commit them (that is, when they were not also encouraging the criminal acts themselves). From the standpoint of Catholics, I am not sure which is worse: a Church and Church leaders morally bankrupt or even criminal because they were so besotted by doctrinal hatred and enmity that they gave their moral blessing to one of the greatest crimes in human history, or a Church and Church leaders morally bankrupt or even criminal because, for their own, perhaps political, reasons, they willfully ignored their duty to warn their members against committing deeds they knew to be criminal, and therefore willfully permitted millions of their members to imperil their souls. . . .

We see then that it is not just the Jewish victims and their families who should be calling for a moral reckoning with the Catholic Church. The call should be coming (and to a small degree is coming) also from Catholics. The Church betrayed its Catholic flock by the tens of millions. Although each one, victimized Jew and morally abandoned Catholic, has a special claim on witnessing such a reckoning, we need not be Jew or Catholic to have a legitimate stake in it. We need not be afflicted Jews or Catholics, or their actual or spiritual descendants. All people have the right, indeed the duty, to engage in moral judgment of significant public events, institutions, and actors. All people have the right and the duty to urge that the conclusions that correctly follow on that moral judgment be widely known and be acted upon. Although such a moral reckoning will serve everyone, no one has a more urgent need for it than the Catholic Church itself, which does not yet know how to call for what it must.

6

| *"The Second Vatican Council [has repudiated] anti-Semitism 'as opposed to the very spirit of Christianity.'"*

Charges of Catholic Anti-Semitism Have Been Exaggerated

David G. Dalin

In the following viewpoint David G. Dalin disputes the contention that the Catholic Church has been a major source of
anti-Semitism in the world. Specifically, he criticizes the
viewpoint of Daniel Jonah Goldhagen, a political scientist
who argues that the church has acknowledged neither its
anti-Semitism nor its culpability for the genocide of European Jews during World War II. Dalin maintains that Goldhagen ignores the fact that Pope Pius XII eagerly assisted
and sheltered persecuted Jews and worked to stop the arrest
and deportation of Jews in Rome. In addition, the author
notes, recent Catholic documents have explicitly denounced
anti-Semitism. Dalin is a rabbi, historian, and scholar of
Christian-Jewish relations. He is the co-editor of *The Pius
War: Responses to the Critics of Pius XII* and the author of the
recently published *The Myth of Hitler's Pope*.

As you read, consider the following questions:
1. What are some of the factual errors contained in
   Goldhagen's book, according to Dalin?
2. What pieces of evidence suggest that Pope Pius XII
   attempted to assist Jews in danger during World War II,
   according to the author?

David G. Dalin, "History as Bigotry," *Weekly Standard*, vol. 8, February 10, 2003,
pp. 38–41.

In its January 21, 2002, issue, the *New Republic* devoted twenty-four pages to Daniel Jonah Goldhagen's "What Would Jesus Have Done?"—one of the most virulent attacks against the Roman Catholic Church ever printed in a major American publication. [In the fall of 2002] Goldhagen expanded that essay into a book, a curious and furious production entitled *A Moral Reckoning: The Role of the Catholic Church in the Holocaust and Its Unfulfilled Duty of Repair*, about the Vatican's role during the Holocaust.

Goldhagen is no stranger to controversy. His 1996 *Hitler's Willing Executioners* argued that blame for the Holocaust should be placed on *all* Germans—for "eliminationist" anti-Semitism was widely spread among prewar Germans and intrinsic to the German character. The Nazi exterminations could occur because the vast majority of Germans were already predisposed to kill Jews. Though Goldhagen gained international celebrity, his book's simplistic argument was widely criticized by serious scholars and historians.

A Vicious Diatribe

In *A Moral Reckoning*, Goldhagen's argument is, once again, simplistic. It's dishonest and misleading as well. He identifies Christianity, and particularly the Catholic Church, as the preeminent source of anti-Semitism in the world—ancient, medieval, and modern. While indicting [Pope] Pius XII as an anti-Semite and a collaborator with Nazi Germany—and ignoring any contradictory evidence—Goldhagen goes on to attribute anti-Semitism to the entire Catholic Church and its leadership, even the [twentieth-century] Church under John Paul II.

Indeed, the book is so flawed—its facts error-prone, its arguments tendentious, and its conclusion, equating Christianity in its essence with anti-Semitism, both bizarre and dangerous—that most scholars in the field have simply tried to ignore it. *Hitler's Willing Executioners* sold very well and was widely praised in its early reviews. *A Moral Reckoning*, however, has flopped badly, despite a large publicity effort by which the publisher Knopf tried to recoup its advance. More prepared this time, reviewers have also been considerably less kind to Goldhagen, and the reviews have generally run from lukewarm to outraged. In the Sunday *Times*, the British historian Michael Burleigh held his nose long enough to brand the book "vile" and "a strip cartoon view of European history."

Despite my fury at Goldhagen's misuse of the Holocaust to advance an anti-Catholic agenda, I had hoped to join the vast conspiracy of silence in which most Holocaust scholars have, delicately and politely, pretended that *A Moral Reckoning* doesn't exist. But the book hasn't quite disappeared with the same speed with which, say, H.G. Wells's 1943 *Crux Ansata: An Indictment of the Roman Catholic Church* fell down the memory hole. Rather, *A Moral Reckoning*—like Paul Blanshard's 1949 diatribe *American Freedom and Catholic Power*—is carving a permanent niche for itself out on the far edges of American culture.

Where Blanshard was a much-reprinted staple for the old anti-Catholic Evangelical world, Goldhagen seems to be turning into a staple for leftists whose hatred of Catholicism derives from the Church's opposition to abortion and the rest of the liberationist agenda. The huge outpouring of books in recent years attacking the wartime pontiff Pius XII—from John Cornwell's *Hitler's Pope* to Garry Wills's *Papal Sin*—were bad enough (and Goldhagen, who seems in *A Moral Reckoning* never to have consulted anything except secondary sources, relies heavily upon them). But when Goldhagen extends that attack to the demand that the Catholic Church, as we know it, be abolished as a disgrace and a danger to us all, he establishes a new marker for just how bad it can get—and the maddened anti-Catholics have responded by taking him to their breast, for his diatribe is more vicious and extreme than that of any other recent papal critic.

Rife with Errors

With all that in mind, it is perhaps worth putting on record some of the failings of *A Moral Reckoning*. Indeed, Goldhagen invites the reader to "acknowledge the incontrovertible facts and plain truths contained in this book." It's an invitation he shouldn't have issued. In the June/July 2002 issue of *First Things*, Ronald J. Rychlak published an extensive and damning list of errors in the *New Republic* article—astonishingly few of which Goldhagen has bothered to correct.

So, for instance, the establishment of the Jewish ghetto in Rome, one of the tragic milestones in the history of Catholic-Jewish relations, took place in 1556, not in 1555; the Venice ghetto in 1517, not 1516; the Frankfurt ghetto in 1462, not 1460; the Vienna ghetto in 1626, not 1570. It's not that these are particularly important errors, but that they are *simple* errors—easy to look up, easy to check. You can't trust anything Goldhagen reports. He is off by three decades about the beginning of the process for Pius XII's beatification. . . .

Then there's the caption that identifies a photo as "Cardinal Michael Faulhaber marches between rows of SA men at a Nazi rally in Munich"—except that the man in the picture isn't Faulhaber but the papal nuncio Cesare Orsenigo, the city isn't Munich but Berlin, and the parade isn't a Nazi rally but a May Day parade. Oh, and the fact that the irascible Faulhaber was a famous opponent of the Nazis. In October [2002], a German court prevented publication of *A Moral Reckoning* until the slander against Faulhaber was corrected.

Ignored Evidence

On and on the factual errors go, the sloppy handling of dates, persons, and places all culminating in the selective use (or ignoring) of evidence to portray Eugenio Pacelli (later Pius XII) as the fount of the era's anti-Semitism. Relying entirely on *Hitler's Pope*, Goldhagen takes what was already an outrageous misreading of a 1919 letter (sent by Pacelli to Rome while serving as papal nuncio in Bavaria) describing a group of Bolshevik revolutionaries who had led an uprising in Munich—which Goldhagen extends to: "The Communist revolutionaries, Pacelli averred in this letter, were 'all' Jews."

The Holy See's 1933 concordat with Germany has long been a key instrument for critics of Pius XII, and indeed there are grounds on which to criticize it. But Goldhagen can't accept mere criticism: "Nazi Germany's first great diplomatic triumph," he has to label it, forgetting that the Four Powers Pact between Germany, France, Italy, and England preceded it, as did League of Nations recognition. Pacelli's concordat "helped to legitimate the Nazi regime in the eyes of the world and consolidate its power at home," Goldhagen insists.

But soon after the concordat was signed, Pacelli wrote two articles in the Vatican newspaper, *L'Osservatore Romano*, unequivocally arguing that the Church had negotiated a treaty and nothing more—a treaty that implied no moral endorsement of Hitler or Nazism. While it's true that Hitler initially thought he would be able to use the concordat to harness the Church, he soon came to regret it—as his frenzied diatribes in his *Table Talk* reveal—precisely because it was being cited by Catholics as a legal basis on which to resist Nazism.

Pope Pius XII Was Not an Anti-Semite

The claim that Pius was an anti-Semite and therefore uninterested in the fate of the Jews stems mainly from his identity as the leader of a church that had promoted anti-Semitism down through the ages; but as an individual, the claim has little factual basis. The specific charge that he was interested only in Jews who had converted to Catholicism is explained by the fact that the Church had a better legal basis to protect those converts. The charge is furthermore not tenable in view of his direct intervention with the Hungarian regent, urging protection for the Jews, and his instruction to his nuncios [diplomats] in the German satellite states to do so as well. He offered to lend the Roman Jews the gold to pay the ransom demanded by the German occupiers. Although specific documentation is lacking, it appears most likely that he directed Italian clergy to open their convents and monasteries to the hunted Jews, and in fact he did open the Vatican's properties to them.

Jose M. Sanchez, *Pius XII and the Holocaust: Understanding the Controversy*, 2002.

Goldhagen's efforts to portray Pacelli as a man whose whole life was fueled by anti-Semitism are made possible only by his ignoring all evidence to the contrary. Guido Mendes, a prominent Italian physician and Pacelli's lifelong Jewish friend, is never mentioned by Goldhagen. Nor is the fact that when Mendes lost his medical professorship as a result of Fascist anti-Semitism, Pacelli personally intervened on his behalf. With Pacelli's direct assistance, Mendes and his family were able to escape and eventually settle in Israel. Pacelli was instrumental in drafting the Vatican's historic 1916 condemnation of anti-Semitism. Bruno Walter, the brilliant Jewish conductor of the Munich Opera whom Pacelli befriended shortly after arriving in Munich in 1917, recounts that Pacelli helped free Walter's Jewish fellow musician, Ossip Gabrilowitsch, who had been imprisoned during a pogrom. These facts are also never mentioned in Goldhagen's one-sided polemic.

Papal Assistance of Persecuted Jews

Goldhagen's centerpiece is the outrageous allegation that Pius XII "did not lift a finger to forfend the deportations of the Jews of Rome" or of other parts of Italy "by instructing his priests and nuns to give the hunted Jewish men, women and children sanctuary." Much of this is lifted straight from anti-Pius books like Susan Zuccotti's *Under His Very Windows*—and thus Goldhagen repeats the errors of those books and adds extras, all his own, in his determined attempt to extend their thesis into over-the-top railings against the sheer existence of Catholicism.

Goldhagen is apparently unaware (or, more probably, doesn't care) that many distinguished scholars have declared Zuccotti's book "not history but guesswork," as the historian Owen Chadwick put it. Zuccotti's principal charge, mindlessly repeated by Goldhagen, is that there is no credible evidence that Pius XII ever explicitly ordered his subordinates to assist Jews in Italy. In fact, there is a whole body of evidence that proves Pius did. In 1964 Cardinal Paolo Dezza, the wartime rector of the Pontifical Gregorian University, published a signed article stating unequivocally that during the German occupation of Rome, Pius XII explicitly told him to help "persecuted Jews" and do so "most willingly." In his 2001 book *Gli ebrei salvati da Pio XII*, Antonio Gaspari compiles additional testimonies. And more recently, Gaspari came across new documents, establishing that as early as 1940 Pius XII explicitly ordered his secretary of state, Luigi Maglione, and Maglione's assistant, Giovanni Battista Montini (the future Paul VI), to send money to Jews protected by the bishop of Campagna.

The Nazi deportations of Italy's Jews began in October 1943. Pope Pius ordered churches and convents throughout Italy to shelter Jews, and in Rome itself 155 convents and monasteries sheltered five thousand Jews throughout the German occupation. Pius himself granted sanctuary within the walls of the Vatican, and his summer residence at Castel Gandolfo, to countless homeless Jews. Goldhagen's book conspicuously lacks any discussion of Castel Gandolfo, which enjoys a unique place in the annals of Jewish rescue (and Catholic rescuers) during the Holocaust: In no other site in all of Nazi-occupied Europe were as many Jews saved and sheltered for as long a period.

The recently released memoirs of Adolf Eichmann also contain new evidence disproving Goldhagen's claim. The memoirs confirm that Vatican protests played a crucial part in obstructing Nazi intentions for Roman Jews. Eichmann wrote that the Vatican "vigorously protested the arrest of Jews, requesting the interruption of such action." At Eichmann's trial in Jerusalem, Israeli attorney general Gideon Hausner said, "the pope himself intervened personally in support of the Jews of Rome." Documents introduced at the trial provide further evidence of Vatican efforts to halt the arrest and deportation of Roman Jews.

Outrageous Accusations

No accusation is too preposterous for Goldhagen to accept. Commenting on the Vatican's alleged link to Nazi war criminals, he claims that Alois Hudal, an Austrian prelate and Nazi sympathizer, was "an important Catholic bishop at the Vatican," as well as a "close friend" and "confidant" of Pius XII. Indeed, he adds, both Pius XII and the future Paul VI actively supported Hudal in his criminal assistance to fleeing Nazi war criminals.

As it happens, Alois Hudal was never a bishop "at the Vatican," much less an "important" one, but rather an obscure rector of the Collegio dell' Anima in Rome, where he was placed to confine him to a post of little significance. Hudal also was never a "close friend" of Pius XII or Montini. In fact, Hudal's memoirs bitterly attack the Vatican for steadfastly refusing an alliance with Nazi Germany to combat "godless Bolshevism." Far from assisting Nazi war criminals in their escape, Pius XII authorized the American Jesuit Edmund Walsh to submit to the War Crimes Tribunal at Nuremberg a dossier documenting Nazi war crimes and atrocities. The recent book by David Alvarez, *Spies in the Vatican: Espionage & Intrigue from Napoleon to the Holocaust*, shows how much Hitler distrusted and despised Pius XII.

An Anti-Catholic Diatribe

Goldhagen's virulent *A Moral Reckoning* focuses on Pius XII as the symbol of Catholic evil and repeats almost every accusation, including the most discredited ones, that has ever been leveled against him. But Goldhagen doesn't limit his anti-Catholic diatribe to Pius. Indeed, the point of all the Holocaust material in *A Moral Reckoning* seems to be the concluding pages' attack on John Paul II and the Catholic Church today. Though Goldhagen begrudgingly acknowledges John Paul II's extraordinary efforts to bring Catholics and Jews closer together, he immediately takes this praise back and ultimately contradicts himself entirely by accusing John Paul II of tolerating "anti-Semitic libels and hatreds" during his visit to Syria in the spring of 2001.

Goldhagen claims that "neither John Paul II nor any other Pope has seen fit to make ... a direct and forceful public statement about Catholics' culpability and the need for all the members of the Church who have sinned during the Holocaust to repent for their many different kinds of offenses and sins against Jews." On the contrary: John Paul II has frequently repented and apologized publicly. In his very first papal audience with Jewish leaders, on March 12, 1979, John Paul II reaffirmed the Second Vatican Council's repudiation of anti-Semitism "as opposed to the very spirit of Christianity," and "which in any case the dignity of the human person alone would suffice to condemn." During his 1986 visit to Rome's chief synagogue—the first time any reigning pope entered a synagogue—John Paul II publicly acknowledged and apologized for the Church's sins. Insisting that there was no theological justification for discrimination, he apologized to the Roman Jews in attendance (many of whom were Holocaust survivors), declaring that the Church condemns anti-Semitism "by anyone—I repeat: by anyone." In 1994, at the personal initiative of John Paul II, the Vatican established diplomatic relations with Israel. In

1998, the Church issued *We Remember: A Reflection on the Shoah*, an official document on the Holocaust. And in 2000, the pope made his historic visit to Israel—one of the great legacies of his pontificate, which has done much to further Catholic-Jewish reconciliation.

But Goldhagen can acknowledge none of this. He identifies Christianity itself as the source of anti-Semitism and declares, "the main responsibility for producing the all-time leading Western hatred lies with Christianity. More specifically, with the Catholic Church." The definition of Jews as Christ-killers, claims Goldhagen, goes back to the origins of Christianity. Indeed, it is still central to Catholic thought today, and it has an "obvious integral relationship to the genesis of the Holocaust."

An Intellectual Scandal

As the Jewish scholar Michael Berenbaum has noted, Goldhagen "omits all mention of the countervailing traditions of tolerance" within Roman Catholic thought, past and present. He also misrepresents the thought of these early Church leaders who advocated a tolerant attitude toward the Jews. Goldhagen's misrepresentation of St. Augustine's views of Jews and Judaism is especially appalling. As Ronald Rychlak has noted, Goldhagen's exposition on St. Augustine "is little more than a crude and contemptuous canard." Similarly, Goldhagen's unsubstantiated claim that "there is no difference in kind between the Church's 'anti-Judaism' and its offshoot European anti-Semitism" is as unsubtle a statement as someone who claims to be a historian could possibly make.

In short, Daniel Jonah Goldhagen's polemic against Pius XII, John Paul II, and the Catholic Church fails to meet even the minimum standards of scholarship. That the book has found its readership out in the fever swamps of anti-Catholicism isn't surprising. But that a mainstream publisher like Knopf would print the thing is an intellectual and publishing scandal.

"The work of the Church's progressive reform movement [is] more important than ever."

Progressive Reformers Are Pushing for Institutional Change

Angela Bonavoglia

The 2002 sex abuse scandal over priests sexually abusing children has outraged Catholics and emboldened many to promote institutional changes that would create a more democratic church, writes Angela Bonavoglia in the following viewpoint. As a result, a small but growing progressive reform movement has taken the lead in challenging the church's stance on several controversial issues, Bonavoglia explains. These reformers promote increased lay involvement in church governance, optional celibacy for priests, contraception, acceptance of homosexuals, academic freedom at Catholic universities, and the inclusion of women at all levels of ministry—including the priesthood. Bonavoglia is a freelance journalist and a contributing editor to *Ms.* magazine.

As you read, consider the following questions:
1. Why did the Vatican try to silence Sister Joan Chittister, according to Bonavoglia?
2. According to sociologist William D'Antonio, cited by the author, what percentage of American Catholics look to the church as a source of moral authority?
3. What is Spiritus Christi, according to Bonavoglia?

Angela Bonavoglia, "The Church's Tug of War," *The Nation*, vol. 275, August 19, 2002, p. 11. Copyright © 2002 by The Nation Magazine/The Nation Company, Inc. Reproduced by permission.

It is a harrowing time for the US Catholic Church. While the American bishops at their Dallas meeting in June [2002] agreed nearly unanimously to remove from active ministry any priest guilty of sexually abusing a minor, they didn't render that decision with enthusiasm. For many, anger and resentment roiled just below the surface.

Take the closing remarks of Chicago's Francis Cardinal George. In an elliptical rant, he held the Church's opponents responsible for the hierarchy's diminishing power. George's targets included the campaign of Catholics for a Free Choice (CFFC) to downgrade the Church's status at the UN [United Nations] to a nongovernmental organization; feminists working for laws requiring Catholic institutions that serve and employ the general public to provide reproductive health services, including contraceptive insurance; anyone suing the Church; Catholics with a shaky faith; Protestants; and American culture in general.

"There's been an erosion of episcopal authority and a loss of Catholic faith for a generation," George scolded. American culture, he said, is "a form of secularized Protestantism . . . self-righteous and decadent at the same time. . . . There's external opposition . . . to the Holy See's being in the United Nations . . . the attack on our healthcare institutes, the attack on our social services through various insurance policies . . . the attack upon our institutional presence that is only beginning . . . as plaintiffs begin to go forward in order to bankrupt the Church. All of these . . . are not coincidental. I believe personally—without looking at it as some kind of cabal . . . that we have to be very serious about how we're going to go forward."

"Going forward" to George means a smaller, more orthodox Church. It would be free of all those "dissidents" who, as the Catholic League's William Donahue has said, "enabled the behavioral deviance." Reflecting similar sentiments, America's cardinals, upon their return from a visit to the Pope in April [2002], issued a statement instructing pastors "clearly to promote the correct moral teaching" and "publicly to reprimand individuals who spread dissent."

One thing is clear from the unprecedented gatherings in Rome and Dallas: If fundamental change is to come to the American Catholic Church, the bishops will not be leading the way. Nor will the Pope, who in Canada recently for World Youth Day finally acknowledged publicly the shame of the sex abuse scandals, but not the hierarchy's culpability. That makes the work of the Church's progressive reform movement more important than ever.

Anne Barrett Doyle is a recent recruit. She says she "literally woke up" in January [2002] when she read the *Boston Globe*'s stories of clergy sex abuse and diocesan cover-up. The same spirit that had moved her as a tenth grader in a packed Roman Catholic Church to protest her priest's refusal to baptize the baby of pro-choice parents inspired her again. Instead of going to their usual parish, she and her family drove to the Cathedral of the Holy Cross, where Bernard Cardinal Law would be serving mass. Carrying her scrawled It's My Church sign, Doyle joined a picket line of seven.

"I was so overcome with the sinfulness of the Church and also of myself, as a lay person who had enjoyed being part of this little club and had not fought against [my] subservient role," says Doyle. Her wake-up call resulted in the birth of one of Boston's most spirited Church reform organizations, the Coalition of Catholics and Survivors. As a leader of that group, Doyle joins the ranks of a largely invisible but driving force behind the Church's progressive change movement: women.

Joan Chittister and the Erie Benedictines

Arguably, the best known is Sister Joan Chittister. A fiery orator and prolific author, this 66-year-old Benedictine nun made international news [in 2001] when she refused to obey a Vatican order forbidding her to speak at an international conference in Dublin on the ordination of women. Chittister made her decision in the face of Vatican threats of "grave penalties," which could have ranged from excommunication to expulsion from her monastery in Erie, Pennsylvania. "The Church that preaches the equality of women but does nothing to demonstrate it within its own structures . . . is . . . dangerously close to repeating the theological errors that underlay centuries of Church-sanctioned slavery," she told the emboldened crowd at the gathering.

Though Chittister would have defied the Pope alone, in

the end, she didn't have to. The Vatican had demanded that the prioress of Chittister's monastery, Christine Vladimiroff, issue the "precept of obedience" forbidding Chittister to speak, or face grave penalties herself. Vladimiroff refused to be the Vatican's henchman. "I could not order something I was in total disagreement with, and that is silencing," says Vladimiroff. Despite advanced age and infirmity, all but one of 128 active members of the Erie Benedictines co-signed Vladimiroff's letter to Rome. An additional letter of support came from nuns in twenty-two other Benedictine communities. The Vatican backed down.

For some, the courage of the Erie Benedictines has been an inspiration. Father Walter Cuenin is a Newton, Massachusetts, parish priest who helped to found another reform group, Priests' Forum. The forum gives Boston priests a private, independent venue to discuss the previously undiscussable—from "whether mandatory celibacy should remain" to Church teachings like the birth-control ban. Cuenin remembers the Benedictines' action well. "It had an impact on me personally," he says. "A lot of us have lived in fear—I can't speak because something will happen. If enough people speak, there's nothing that anyone can do."

Catholics Are Ready for Reform

There is no question that the pedophilia scandal has torn the mantle of sanctity off the Catholic Church. Long subject to a litany of illogical and unconscionable sexual prohibitions—which the Church labors worldwide to have written into secular law—Catholics now see that the hierarchy has failed to live up to even the most basic moral standards. That, explains Catholic University sociologist William D' Antonio, has exacerbated their outrage. His research revealed that only 20 percent of American Catholics look to Church leaders as a source of moral authority, and that was before the scandals broke. Most also believe that the Church should be more democratic. "What our data show," D'Antonio says, "is that people are ready for the reform movement.". . .

In the spirit of the Second Vatican Council (1962–65), the progressive reform groups embrace a broad agenda. They want women at all levels of ministry and decision-making;

married clergy; optional celibacy; acceptance of homosexuals, the divorced and the remarried; an end to Vatican silencings; lay involvement in Church governance and in teachings on human sexuality (though abortion support varies, even among reformers); new forms of liturgy and nonsexist language; academic freedom at Catholic universities; and an affirmation of conscience as the final arbiter in moral matters.

Luckovich. © 2001 by Creators Syndicate, Inc. Reproduced by permission.

This agenda is embraced by such groups as Call to Action—the nation's oldest and largest, with 25,000 members and forty chapters; the gay rights group Dignity/USA; the Women's Ordination Conference; the reproductive rights groups CFFC and Catholics Speak Out; Corpus, which supports married and female priests; Women-Church Convergence, a coalition committed to feminist spirituality; and FutureChurch, which raises awareness of the priest shortage and of women's ministerial roles in the early and the contemporary Church. All are led or co-led by women.

By contrast, the new "center" is occupied by reformers with a narrower agenda. Like the progressive groups, they support the long-neglected victims of clergy sexual abuse—represented by the Survivors Network of Those Abused by Priests (SNAP) and Linkup. But they call for change in only one area: Church governance. They want the hierarchy to share power, giving lay Catholics a real voice in administrative affairs such as financial decision-making and the hiring and firing of priests and bishops. Another new group, Voice of the Faithful [VOTF] in Boston, is working swiftly and systematically to move the agenda of Church accountability forward. With 22,500 members in forty states and twenty-two countries, VOTF is building an exploding network of independent, parish-based groups. In addition, VOTF has set up a charitable fund through which Catholics can redirect their donations from Boston's archdiocesan coffers to Catholic agencies—the only real power Catholics currently have. . . .

The Depths of the Crisis

As for the progressive reformers, they see in the current crisis dramatic evidence of the need for change. They are incensed by the hierarchy's scapegoating of homosexual priests as the cause of the scandals. In fact, they point out, that contention cannot be separated from the Church's denial of the rampant sexual abuse of girls and women by Catholic priests, which some contend far outstrips the abuse of male children in its incidence. Half the members of both SNAP and Linkup are women. [In 2001] internal Church documents revealed a pattern of sexual abuse and exploitation of nuns—and other girls and women—by priests in some twenty-three countries, on five continents. What's more, according to the research of psychotherapist and former Catholic monk Richard Sipe, at any one time, at least a third of priests, regardless of sexual orientation, are sexually active with adults. Whether those relationships are exploitative or consensual, they indicate the depth of the hypocrisy inherent in the claim of a celibate priesthood.

Progressive reformers see women's overall subordinate role in the Church—including the ban on ordination—as contributing to this crisis. Another Call to Action spokeswoman, Linda Pieczynski, suggests that if women—particularly mothers—had been at the table, "We wouldn't have tried to save Father Bob's reputation. We would have protected the children." Indeed, we have seen how women in male-dominated institutions—Sherron Watkins at Enron, Coleen Rowley at the FBI—have blown the lid off secret shenanigans. But integrating women into positions of power in the Church means taking on an issue absent from the public dialogue: misogyny. As Chittister has observed, the Roman Church "built a bad theology of male superiority on a bad biology that defined women as passive incubators of male sperm . . . inferior by nature and deficient of soul, the servants of men and the seducers of civilization."

Breakaway Reformers

While reformers in the new middle are trying to force the hierarchy to share power, plenty of progressive reformers have chosen to go their own way, while continuing obstinately to call themselves Catholic. [In November 2001] Mary Ramerman lay prostrate on a stage before 3,000 jubilant supporters in Rochester, New York's Eastman Theatre, where she was ordained a Catholic priest. While Ramerman was ordained in the Old Catholic rather than the Roman Catholic Church (the Old Catholics broke with Rome when it declared the doctrine of papal infallibility in 1870), she took that action against the orders of Rochester Bishop Matthew Clark, who directed her "to abandon your leadership role" at Spiritus Christi. A vigorous congregation of 1,500, Spiritus grew out of the smoldering ashes of another Catholic parish, Corpus Christi. That was after Clark dismissed both its pastor, in part for allowing Ramerman on the altar during mass, and Ramerman for refusing to step off.

"They are a real problem [for the Catholic Church] because that's the most alive faith community in that whole area," says Sister Maureen Fiedler, advisory board member of Catholics Speak Out and host of the radio show Interfaith Voices. CFFC president Frances Kissling agrees. "What is the best example of Church reform in the United States right now? Spiritus Christi. They have a vital, lively church that is not connected to the institution, but that views itself as Catholic."

Revving up the rebellion, on June 29 [2002], seven

women—four Germans, two Austrians and one with dual Austrian-American citizenship—were ordained Roman Catholic priests on a cruise ship, the MS Passau, on the Danube River, just outside of Passau, Germany. Romulo Braschi of Argentina was the presiding bishop. While Braschi was ordained a Catholic priest and later, a bishop, he leads a splinter sect and has no standing with the Vatican. As a result, some reformers distanced themselves from the ordination. Others, like Fiedler, who attended, saw it as an important step forward. "I think what Rome worries about is that this could start breaking out all over," she says.

Intentional Communities

While much smaller than Spiritus Christi—some have only a handful of members—hundreds of Catholic intentional eucharistic communities exist around the country. In the tradition of the early Christian church and Latin America's small base communities, these worship communities—some decades old—meet regularly, often in people's homes; celebrate the eucharist, with their own liturgies; and choose their own worship leaders, including married Catholic priests, openly gay Catholic priests and Catholic women.

Reformers also labor outside the Church to curb its power in the world. No group has worked longer to challenge the institutional Church's attempts to restrict access to reproductive healthcare than Catholics for a Free Choice (I served for a time on CFFC's board). More recently, secular women's groups have joined in this work.

After toiling in near-obscurity, progressive Church reform groups have been hurled by the current crisis into the spotlight. They report increased hits on their websites, more calls and letters, jumps in membership, more donations. Though their membership rosters remain very low, considering that the country has 63 million Catholics, there is a lot of talk about the demand for Church reform finally having reached critical mass. . . .

The Role of the Laity

The progress to be made, in the end, depends on the will of the laity. "Catholics need to get much more vocal with the diocesan leadership about what kinds of things they're going to tolerate and what kinds of things they're not," says FutureChurch executive director Sister Chris Schenk. "And they're going to have to link it to the pocketbook." That's a special challenge for devout Catholics used to obeying, and for so-called cafeteria Catholics, who may feel little responsibility for the institutional Church.

As to how quickly change will come, Chittister offers a perspective. "I'm talking about the movement of tectonic plates," she says, reflecting on the magnitude of the challenges ahead. "I am not talking about tiny, little organizational cosmetics, a new set of rules for how we report on something. I'm talking about a whole institutional Church, about the conversion of this clerical institution into a real Church society."

"More of my peers . . . are returning not merely to traditional ways of thinking, but in a remarkable number of cases, to the orthodox Christianity many of their parents rejected in their youth."

Observant Youths Are Returning to Established Traditions

Bronwen Catherine McShea

In the following viewpoint Bronwen Catherine McShea contends that a growing number of young Catholics are embracing Christian orthodoxy and traditional church teachings. Unlike the older, liberal Catholics who seek to usurp church authority, these young, observant Catholics are inspired by the church's traditional stance on faith, natural law, sexuality, and family life, McShea points out. This youthful return to ancient church wisdom includes a rejection of abortion, an opposition to women's ordination, and the celebration of procreative marriage as a sacrament, the author maintains. McShea was a candidate in the Master of Theological Studies program at Harvard Divinity School when she wrote this essay.

As you read, consider the following questions:
1. According to Father Paul McNellis, how should young Catholics fight "the evil of abortion"?
2. What are the church's countercultural messages, in McShea's opinion?
3. What church teaching makes the beauty of orthodoxy especially apparent, in McShea's view?

Bronwen Catherine McShea, "Harvard Springtime," *First Things*, August/September 2003, p. 12. Copyright © 2003 by the Institute on Religion and Public Life. Reproduced by permission.

On Sunday, April 27 [2003], one of the large lecture halls at Harvard Divinity School was two-thirds filled primarily with graying, upper-middle-class liberal women of the baby-boom generation who had come to hear and applaud Dr. Ida Raming's "courageous" story of resisting the all-male hierarchy of the Roman Catholic Church. Raming, you may recall, is one of seven women, mostly German and Austrian, who were excommunicated in summer 2002 for participating in an illicit ordination ceremony. She celebrated a liturgy at Harvard, kindling the activist fires in her supportive listeners, who are working to "liberate" women from the Roman "structures of power" that have discriminated against them these long twenty centuries.

One expects such fare at Harvard. It was not twenty-four hours earlier, however, that Richard John Neuhaus addressed a crowd three times as large at the nearby Harvard Law School campus—a crowd consisting largely of young, conservative Catholic graduate students and professionals, evenly divided by sex, and of visibly diverse ethnic backgrounds. Here, Neuhaus elicited a standing ovation upon encouraging our generation to continue answering God's call to fight the evil of abortion in America—"the great civil rights issue of our time." He reminded us that the Catholic Church has been the voice crying out in the wilderness on this issue as on many others. His talk followed another by Father Paul McNellis of Boston College's philosophy department, who tied the abortion issue to that of sexuality, telling the sympathetic crowd that one way to fight the evil of abortion on the personal level is for young men to start living chastely out of a "courageous," "manly" protectiveness toward young women —to love their girlfriends truly and stop leading them into situations in which abortion is a temptation.

Liberals Versus Traditionalists

The aspirations of these two crowds could not have been more different. Since the 1960s, the first crowd has sought to seize power from the leaders of the Catholic Church, to recast the Church in the image of modern, liberal society, and to purge it of all distinctions, not only between male and female, but also between priest and people, and even between mankind and God Himself. By contrast, the second crowd turns away from the moral and philosophical confusions of the sixties toward the leaders of the Church—particularly toward a Pope who asserts without blushing his divinely ordained authority to define what is right and wrong. They embrace a view of the world that has a privileged place for lasting and binding conceptions of natural and divine law, and for the traditional authorities that continue to expound such teachings despite the world's resounding rejection of them.

Having been a student at Harvard for five years—first as an undergraduate, now as a Master's candidate in religious studies—I have observed a growing chasm between the aspirations of the generation that is teaching us and those of more and more of my peers who are returning not merely to traditional ways of thinking, but in a remarkable number of cases, to the orthodox Christianity many of their parents rejected in their youth. While it would be misleading to say that such students make up anything more than a small minority at Harvard, their numbers are undeniably growing, in large part because of their infectiously hopeful spirit.

Within my own immediate circle of friends at school, for example, there are at least a dozen who either have converted to orthodox Catholicism from other faiths or from no faith at all, or embraced such Catholicism on their own despite having been raised in lax Catholic homes. Each of them has additional friends with similar stories. Friends who have previously been students at Princeton, Yale, and elsewhere have spoken of similar phenomena on those campuses. Having been raised myself in an unusually strong Catholic home where one often felt like a member of a dying race, I have been swept off my feet these past few years by the enthusiasm of friends who have come to the faith—especially its moral teachings—despite its extremely countercultural messages.

Young Faithful Catholics

The presence of these young, faithful Catholics was particularly evident this spring [of 2003] at Harvard. Student attendance has been significant at daily masses, regular Confession, and Rosary groups both at the College and at the Law School.

In addition to the annual symposium on pro-life issues put on by the Harvard Society for Law, Life, and Religion, as well as the ongoing activities of the undergraduate pro-life organization, Harvard Right to Life, Catholic students at Harvard have benefited from discussion groups on Thomas Aquinas, natural law, and the women doctors of the Church. Participants in these groups confidently and cheerfully embrace orthodoxy and the teachings of the Magisterium.[1]

The Path Back to Rome

Gen-Xers may be starting a trend—young people making their own way back to Rome [the Roman Catholic Church], despite misguided teachers. After a generation or two of malformation, today's young Catholics still have an appetite for what the Church offers. Colleen Carroll, author of *The New Faithful: Embracing Christian Orthodoxy*, spent the last few years interviewing young Christians. She says, "A fair number of the young adults I interviewed for my book labeled themselves 'reverts'—those who left the Church consciously, or simply fell away, then had powerful conversion experiences that led them back to the Church." In many of their cases, they left as teenagers who were turned away by what they often cited as "spiritually dead worship." Increasingly, though, they're finding lively fellowship and community worship focused on the Eucharist—something very different from their childhood experiences of the Faith.

Kathryn Jean Lopez, "Why Young Catholics Leave the Church and How to Bring Them Back," *Crisis*, December 2002.

Moreover, a graduate and professional student Bible study group has sprung up; every week fifteen to twenty students gather to discuss the gospel and to integrate it with insights drawn from Pope John Paul II's encyclicals, writings of the doctors of the Church, and lessons from the Church Fathers. Perhaps the most public and successful event was the coming of a "Theology on Tap" series to a bar in Harvard Square, where large numbers of young people in the area gathered regularly to hear informal but very well-informed and inspirational talks by orthodox Catholic priests and laymen. The series will be returning to Cambridge [in the fall of 2003].

1. The Magisterium is the teaching authority of the Church, which is vested in the pope and the bishops.

Embracing Traditional Theology

What I find particularly striking about many of my peers in this veritable young Catholic movement at Harvard—particularly the young women among them—is their fervent rejection of modern liberal conceptions of sexual difference, sexual relations, and family life. They are familiar with Pope John Paul II's "Theology of the Body," for example, and embrace warmly the message of encyclicals such as *Evangelium Vitae* and *Humanae Vitae*. They also support the Church's stance that women cannot be ordained as priests, seeing in it a recognition that men and women—having distinct natures, body and soul, and complementing one another in a way that reflects a higher theological reality—ought to continue to have separate roles within the life of the Church.

To flesh out further the countercultural intellectual orientation of some of these young women, it is useful to point out the popularity among them of Professors Mary Ann Glendon of Harvard Law School and Harvey C. Mansfield, Jr. of the Harvard government department. Glendon, a member of the Pontifical Council for the Laity, has been an outstanding inspiration for these women, who are looking to role models who combine success with faithful Catholicism. Mansfield (who is not himself Catholic) has been awakening students for decades to premodern, particularly Aristotelian views of natural right, and he is currently making waves in academe, particularly among feminists, with a project on manliness, arguing that the social and philosophical reality of sexual differences may be more fundamental than our officially gender-blind society allows itself to see.

The Beauty of Orthodoxy

The more cynical of the older women who attended Ida Raming's talk at Harvard Divinity School would probably trace my opinions to the subtle enslavement of our sex by men (chief among them the charismatic Pope John Paul II). Yet I and many of my peers can only shake our heads in wonder at the blindness of so many in the sixties' generation to the beauty of orthodoxy. This beauty is particularly apparent to us in the Church's teachings on sexuality: these teachings seem to express a sublime reality that we catch glimpses of in our own lives—in observing and relating to young men, and in our continual journey with Jesus Christ toward God the Father. Human masculinity and femininity have their own loveliness in relation to one another, reflecting the mystical romance between Christ and his Church. To ordain women to the priesthood—to robe them in the trappings of those who truly act in persona Christi in the sacramental life of the Church—seems to us to upset the harmonious order of the universe at which we have learned to gaze in wonder, despite all the obstacles to such visions presented by our dreary modern world. Likewise, we are learning to see again the beauty of marriage conceived as a sacrament, and openness to new life within marriage as the due thanks we must give to God for the privilege He grants us to participate in His creative power through procreation.

My generation is increasingly catching glimpses of the beauty of a society that is committed in spirit and in law to a culture of life, which is why we are turning against abortion. There is no turning back when one beholds such beauty—when one falls in love with God's will for the human family. We recognize the struggles that accompany acting upon a commitment to His will, but such struggles appeal to the idealistic impulses of youth. They are hurdles to be scaled, not avoided.

These are exciting times for the Catholic Church in America, as the eventful April weekend at Harvard proved to me and my friends in abundance. There is a generational struggle afoot, and it is not at all what the 1960s generation would have predicted it would be. Young men and women are turning to the ancient wisdom of the Church—even at Harvard University.

Periodical Bibliography

The following articles have been selected to supplement the diverse views presented in this chapter.

Tom Bethell — "Catholicism in Crisis," *American Spectator*, January/February 2003.

Joan Chittister — "'The Faith Will Survive': The Institutional Church, on the Other Hand, Is in Serious Trouble. Here's Why," *Sojourners*, July/August 2002.

H.W. Crocker III — "What's So Great About Catholicism," *Crisis*, November 2002.

Charles E. Curran — "The Pope's Passions," *Christian Century*, November 15, 2003.

Edd Doerr — "Split Personality," *Humanist*, May/June 2002.

Jay P. Dolan — "To Form a More Perfect Union," *U.S. Catholic*, October 2003.

Paul Elie — "A Church in Search of Followers," *New York Times*, June 23, 2003.

Andrew Greeley — "Young Fogeys: Young Reactionaries, Aging Radicals—the U.S. Catholic Church's Unusual Clerical Divide," *Atlantic Monthly*, January/February 2004.

Richard P. McBrien — "Red and Blue Catholics and More: U.S. Catholic Church Has at Least Three Constituencies," *National Catholic Reporter*, October 29, 2004.

Richard Neuhaus — "The Persistence of the Catholic Moment," *First Things*, February 2003.

Robert Scheer — "Flicking Fallen Angels Off the Head of a Pin," *Los Angeles Times*, June 18, 2002.

Bret Schulte and Rochelle Sharpe — "Struggling to Keep the Faith," *U.S. News & World Report*, December 27, 2004.

Donald Senior — "Rome Has Spoken: A New Catholic Approach to Judaism," *Commonweal*, January 31, 2003.

Russell Shaw — "Ignoring the Obvious: The Unreality of American Catholicism," *Crisis*, March 2003.

Margaret Spillane — "The People's Church," *Nation*, January 6, 2003.

What Led to the Sex Abuse Scandal in the Catholic Church?

Chapter Preface

In 2002 the Roman Catholic Church in the United States was faced with its greatest crisis to date as numerous disclosures of child sexual abuse by its priests came to light. Those in the archdiocese of Boston, Massachusetts, were deeply disturbed to discover that several priests had remained in parish posts for decades despite a history of acknowledged child molestation. Throughout the ensuing months, other dioceses across the nation were shaken by similar revelations about priests and sexual abuse. Catholics and non-Catholics alike were stunned to learn that the church hierarchy had repeatedly mishandled the problem by neglecting to report abusive priests to civil authorities and by re-assigning these priests to ministries involving youths. Moreover, 2002 was not the first year that the U.S. Catholic Church had been embroiled in a sex-abuse crisis. During the 1980s and the 1990s, a series of sex-abuse allegations led to numerous lawsuits and convictions of priests. For many observers the 2002 scandal proves that church authorities had never taken the necessary steps to protect minors from abusive clergy despite the problem's reoccurrence.

As experts examine the factors that may have contributed to the most recent crisis, they often note that the majority of publicized cases involve a priest's sexual contact with adolescent males. This has prompted many people to question the role that homosexuality plays in clerical sexual misconduct. While the Catholic Church teaches that homosexual activity is immoral and that same-sex attraction is "disordered," a homosexual orientation in itself is not considered sinful. Thus, the Catholic clergy has not officially excluded gay men, and various surveys have estimated that anywhere from 2 to 50 percent of priests are homosexual. Catholic psychologist Joseph Nicolosi believes that homosexuality in the priesthood is a significant contributing factor in the sex abuse crisis. "My clinical experience convinces me that a man with a homosexual orientation has greater difficulty controlling his sexuality and is more inclined to obsessive-compulsive tendencies," Nicolosi argues. In addition, he claims that "there is a greater tendency for a homosexual to sexually engage himself with a youth, a minor, or a preteen or early teen boy." Theologian George Weigel agrees: "Gays have a very difficult time living chastely," he contends. "[So] it seems to me that the church ought to be very, very careful about ordaining gay men. I would say the exact same thing about ordaining heterosexuals who have shown an inability to live chaste lives."

But many analysts strongly disagree with these conclusions about gay priests. Most psychologists discount the notion that homosexuality is linked to sexual abuse. Frederick Berlin, a Johns Hopkins psychiatry professor who specializes in sexual disorders, contends that "there is no evidence whatsoever that pedophilia occurs more frequently among homosexuals" than among heterosexuals and that "homosexuals are no more risk to children than heterosexuals." Some observers see the focus on the homosexual issue as a way for critics to scapegoat gay clergy and eventually exclude gay men from the priesthood. Religion scholar Mark Jordan believes that this would be a mistake in a church that has seen a drastic decline in priestly vocations over the past four decades. "If you could fire all the gay priests tomorrow," says Jordan, "you would so greatly reduce the number of priests that the church could no longer function." Instead of casting the blame on homosexuality, many experts maintain that society needs to examine why adult men, straight or gay, sexually abuse minors and why church authorities have repeatedly mishandled or covered up such crimes.

In the following chapter authors speculate further about the potential causes and contributing factors underlying the sex abuse scandal in the Catholic Church.

*"If there were few homosexuals in the
priesthood, the number of sex-abuse victims
today would be drastically lower."*

Homosexuality in the Priesthood Contributes to Child Sexual Abuse

Rod Dreher

The growing number of homosexuals in the priesthood is related to the increasing incidents of child sexual abuse in the Catholic Church, argues Rod Dreher in the following viewpoint. Most victims have actually been teenage males, suggesting that the problem is not really rooted in pedophilia (sexual abuse of prepubescent children) but in homosexuality, Dreher maintains. He contends that a network of gay clergy, including those who have influence in seminaries and in the hierarchy, helped to undermine the church's traditional teachings on sexual morality and ultimately created a climate conducive to sexual abuse. Dreher is a senior writer for the *National Review*, a conservative journal of news and opinion.

As you read, consider the following questions:

1. Why is it difficult to determine the number of gay men in the priesthood, according to Dreher?
2. According to the author, what is the Catholic Church's official policy on homosexuality?
3. What should the Catholic Church do to prevent sexual abuse by clergy, in Dreher's opinion?

Rod Dreher, "The Gay Question: Amid the Catholic Church's Current Scandals, an Unignorable Issue," *National Review*, vol. 43, April 22, 2002, pp. 35–37. Copyright © 2002 by National Review, Inc., 215 Lexington Ave., New York, NY 10016. Reproduced by permission.

The first thing to understand about the Catholic Church's pedophilia scandal is that it is not technically a pedophilia scandal. Despite the gruesome example of defrocked Boston priest John Geoghan, whose case started the current tidal wave of revelations, the overwhelming majority of priests who have molested minors are not pedophiles—that is, like Geoghan, among the rare adults sexually attracted to prepubescent children. They are, rather, "ephebophiles"—adults who are sexually attracted to post-pubescent youths, generally aged 12 to 17. And their victims have been almost exclusively boys.

Stephen Rubino, a New Jersey lawyer, says that of the over 300 alleged victims of priest sex abuse he has represented, roughly 85 percent are boys, and were teenagers when the abuse occurred. Dr. Richard Fitzgibbons, an eminent Catholic psychiatrist who has treated scores of victims and priest-perpetrators, says 90 percent of his patients were either teen male victims of priests, or priests who abused teen boys.

"I think we have to ask the question: Why are 90 percent to 95 percent, and some estimates say as high as 98 percent, of the victims of clergy [abuse] teenage boys? . . . We need to ask that question, and I think there's a certain reluctance to raise that issue," said the Rev. Donald B. Cozzens, author of *The Changing Face of the Priesthood*, on a recent *Meet the Press*.

The Man Behind the Curtain

The reluctance arises, no doubt, partly out of a fear of antagonizing homosexual anti-defamation groups, who resent the stereotype of male homosexuals as pederasts. It's much safer to focus inquiry on the question of mandatory celibacy, or the issue of ordaining women. Yet it defies common sense to imagine that an ordinary man, having made a vow not to marry, is therefore going to be sexually attracted to boys. Indeed, suppose the Second Vatican Council in the 1960s had admitted married men to the ranks of the Catholic priesthood: Would a single adolescent boy molested over the past 40 years have escaped his fate? Similarly, if women had been ordained, would that somehow have made sexually predatory gay priests disappear?

No, this is chiefly a scandal about unchaste or criminal

homosexuals in the Catholic priesthood, and about far too many in Church leadership disinclined to deal with the problem—or, worse, who may in some cases be actively involved in the misconduct. For Catholics, to start asking questions about homosexuality in the priesthood is to risk finding out more than many Church members prefer to know. For journalists, to confront the issue is to risk touching the electrified third rail of American popular culture: the dark side of homosexuality. Yet when we learn that the greatest crisis the Catholic Church in America has ever faced has been brought upon it almost wholly by male clerics seducing boys, attention must be paid to the man behind the curtain.

It is true that a great many gay people are sickened and appalled by what these wicked priests have done to boys, and some with a public voice, like journalist Andrew Sullivan, have vigorously denounced it. At the same time, Sullivan has strongly supported the ministry of gay priests.

How Many Priests Are Gay?

How many gay priests are there? No one can say with certainty; the American bishops have never formally studied the issue, and, for obvious reasons, it is all but impossible to determine an accurate number. Richard Sipe, a laicized priest and psychotherapist who has studied the phenomenon of priests and sex abuse for most of his 40-year career, believes 20 percent of Catholic priests are homosexual, and that half of those are sexually active. In his book, Fr. Cozzens cites various studies putting the total much higher, but these surveys typically suffer from methodological problems that skew the numbers upward.

But those who lowball the numbers could equally be accused of wanting to downplay the problem. The Rev. C. John McCloskey, a member of the conservative Opus Dei organization, claimed recently that the number of gay priests is "two percent to four percent at a maximum," or equivalent to the estimated number of homosexuals in the general population; if that were true, however, it would be hard to explain why, according to experts, Catholic priests are dying of AIDS at a higher rate than males in the general population.

A Network of Militant Homosexuals

The raw numbers are less important, though, if homosexual priests occupy positions of influence in the vast Catholic bureaucracy; and there seems little doubt that this is the case in the American Church. Lest this be dismissed as right-wing paranoia, it bears noting that psychotherapist Sipe is no conservative—indeed, he is disliked by many on the Catholic Right for his vigorous dissent from Church teaching on sexual morality—yet he is convinced that the sexual abuse of minors is facilitated by a secret, powerful network of gay priests. Sipe has a great deal of clinical and research experience in this field; he has reviewed thousands of case histories of sexually active priests and abuse victims. He is convinced of the existence of what the Rev. Andrew Greeley, the left-wing clerical gadfly, has called a "lavender Mafia."

"This is a system. This is a whole community. You have many good people covering it up," Sipe says. "There is a network of power. A lot of seminary rectors and teachers are part of it, and they move to chancery-office positions, and on to bishoprics. It's part of the ladder of success. It breaks your heart to see the people who suffer because of this."

In his new book, *Goodbye! Good Men*, Michael S. Rose documents in shocking detail how pervasive militant homosexuality is in many seminaries, how much gay sex is taking place among seminarians and priest-professors, and how gay power cliques exclude and punish heterosexuals who oppose them. "It's not just a few guys in a few seminaries that have an ax to grind. It is a pattern," says Rose. "The protective network [of homosexual priests] begins in the seminaries."

The stories related in Rose's book will strike many as incredible, but they track closely with the stories that priests have told me about open gay sex and gay politicking in seminaries. The current scandal is opening Catholic eyes: As one ex-seminarian says, "People thought I was crazy when I told them what it was like there, so I finally quit talking about it. They're starting to see now that I wasn't."

Goodbye! Good Men links homosexuality among priests with theological dissent, a connection commonly made by conservative Catholics who wonder why their parish priests have practically abandoned teaching and explaining Catholic sexual morality. But one veteran vocations-team member for a conservative diocese cautions that Catholics should not assume that theological orthodoxy guarantees heterosexuality or chastity. "You find [active homosexuality] among some pretty conservative orders, and in places you'd not expect it," he says. "That's what makes this so depressing. You don't know where to turn."

An especially nasty aspect of this phenomenon is the vulnerability of sexually active gay priests and bishops to manipulation via blackmail. Priests, psychiatrists, and other informed parties say they encounter this constantly. "It's the secrecy," says Stephen Rubino. "If you're a bishop and you're having a relationship, and people know about it, are you compromised on dealing with sexually abusive priests? You bet you are. I've seen it happen."

Homosexuality and Abuse

Q: How much of an overlap is there between homosexuality and pedophilia?

A: The fact is, there is a higher correlation between homosexuality and pedophilia than there is between heterosexuality and pedophilia. The popular media and certainly "gay" apologists are denying this vehemently. But the fact is, there is a greater tendency for a homosexual to sexually engage himself with a youth, a minor, or a preteen or early teen boy.

There are multiple studies to support this. And in the childhoods of both homosexuals and lesbians, we see that an alarming proportion have been victims of abuse themselves. Male victims of abuse, in particular, are more likely to repeat the abuse when they become adults.

Joseph Nicolosi, *Wanderer*, June 27, 2002.

Longtime observers predict that . . . bishops and priests will be forced to resign under fire after their closeted homosexual lives, including sexual abuse, become public. The disgraced pederast former bishop of Palm Beach, Fla., is probably not alone. If this happens, the Vatican will face mounting pressure from the Catholic rank-and-file to take action. As Fr. Greeley has written, "The laity, I suspect, would say it is one thing to accept a homosexual priest and quite another to accept a substantially homosexual clergy, many of whom are blatantly part of the gay subculture."

Examining Church Policy

Rome has explicitly discouraged the ordination of homosexuals since at least 1961. For the past decade, the Vatican has been ratcheting up the pressure against gay ordination—to little avail in most U.S. dioceses. [In 2001] Archbishop Tarcisio Bertone, a top Vatican official, said gays should not be admitted to seminaries, a line that was reinforced in early March [2002] by the Pope's spokesman, Joaquin Navarro-Valls. Recent reports indicate that the Vatican may soon release another document to restate and clarify this policy.

Today, those who defend allowing homosexuals into the priesthood point to the Church's official teaching, which distinguishes between homosexual orientation (which the Church does not consider sinful) and homosexual acts (which the Catechism labels "grave depravity"). There is nothing wrong, the argument goes, with ordaining a homosexually oriented man committed to living chastely and to upholding the Church's teaching on sexuality. Surely there are many such faithful priests in service.

This argument, though, seems persuasive only under conditions far removed from those under which priests have to live today. We now have a culture in which there is little support for chastity, even from within the ranks of the Catholic priesthood. Conservative theologian Michael Novak says he is not prepared to argue for the exclusion of homosexuals from ordination, but as an ex-seminarian, he strongly believes gays should not be on seminary faculties, directing the formation in chastity of young men. Other Catholics who are more liberal than Novak on many Church issues go further on the question of gay ordination: Sipe believes gays shouldn't be admitted into seminaries at the present time—for their own protection, against sexual predators among the faculty and administration, who will attempt to draw them into a priestly subculture in which gay sex is normative behavior. Fr. Thomas P. Doyle, another critic of celibacy who has been deeply involved in the clergy-abuse issue, concurs: "Ordaining gay men at this time would be putting them, no matter how good and dedicated, in a precarious position."

Learning Significant Lessons

No one wants to stigmatize homosexuals as abusers, because most of them are not. Still, it's hard to gainsay the contention that if there were few homosexuals in the priesthood, the number of sex-abuse victims today would be drastically lower. "We're learning a significant lesson from all this," says Dr. Fitzgibbons. "We have to protect our young. The protection of children and teenagers is more important than the feelings of homosexuals."

Though the American scandal is nowhere near played out, it seems likely that the barrage of humiliating revelations and mounting financial losses will force the Vatican to get tough on gay ordinations. To have any hope of being effective, Rome will have to clean house at most American seminaries. This can be done only if local bishops can be trusted to be both loyal to Rome and resolute—and that will happen only if the Vatican forces them to be accountable.

That still leaves the problem of current and future priests who are both homosexual and unchaste. It is true that most of the abuse cases that have reached the public's attention today involve older priests, and the situation in the seminaries has apparently been reined in somewhat from the anything-goes heyday of the 1970s and 1980s. Nevertheless, the problem is still enormous. Most of the cases reported in *Goodbye! Good Men* involving homosexual corruption date from recent years. One priest who left his seminary teaching post in the mid 1990s in despair over rampant homosexuality—and episcopal indifference to it—told me ominously: "The things I have seen in my years there are probably previews of coming attractions."

Curing the Church's Ills

The only sensible response, it would seem, is a zero-tolerance policy when it comes to sexual behavior by clergy, even between consenting adults (homosexual and heterosexual). The laity has a role to play as well. In a much-discussed essay in the November 2000 *Catholic World Report*, the Rev.

Paul Shaughnessy, a Jesuit priest, suggested that lay Catholics seeking reform should help keep their priests accountable. He urged lay Catholics to use their checkbooks to fight sexual corruption, by steering their donations away from scandal-ridden dioceses and religious orders, and sending them instead to clean groups like Mother Teresa's Missionaries of Charity—and then letting the bishop or religious order know what they've done and why.

There is tremendous fear among churchmen that the kind of changes needed to put the Church aright will result in a severe loss of numbers in the priesthood at a time when vocations are already at a historic low. That is probably true in the short run, but the experience of a handful of American dioceses in which the local bishop is openly orthodox and willing to defend Church teaching without compromise gives reason to hope that a strong dose of traditional medicine can go a long way toward curing the Church's ills.

In 1995, Archbishop Elden Curtiss of Omaha published an article pointing out that dioceses that promote rigorous fidelity to Church teaching and practice produce significantly more vocations than do the moderate to liberal majority. Seminaries like Mount Saint Mary's in Emmitsburg, Md.—where men know they will be supported in their authentic Catholic beliefs and practices, and in their commitment to celibacy and chastity—are filled to capacity.

This is not to suggest that the crisis now gripping the Catholic Church in America can be entirely solved by a restoration of rigorously orthodox theology. Another problem that has to be addressed is the clericalist bias seriously afflicting the judgment of many bishops: Even Curtiss himself erred recently, by keeping an Omaha priest in ministry after the priest admitted having a child-pornography problem. But a return to the basics has to be a big part of a comprehensive solution. There is every reason to believe that a conservative reform—replacing dissenting or milquetoast bishops with solid, no-nonsense men; making the seminaries safe places for heterosexuals loyal to Church teaching; and restoring the priesthood to a corps of chaste, faith-filled disciples—would result in a tide of good men seeking holy orders.

This has already been happening in dioceses like Omaha;

Lincoln, Neb.; Denver; Peoria, Ill.; Fargo, ND., and Arlington, Va. The road map that points the way to an authentic renewal of the Catholic priesthood is being drawn up in those places. And if you want to see the alternative—what would happen if the U.S. Church simply stayed on its current course—just read the morning papers.

"All this must stop: the scapegoating of gay priests for the sex abuse crisis [and] the demand to reject homosexual persons for the priesthood and religious life."

Homosexuality in the Priesthood Does Not Contribute to Child Sexual Abuse

Thomas J. Gumbleton

Homosexuality in the priesthood has no connection to child sexual abuse in the Catholic Church, argues Thomas J. Gumbleton in the following viewpoint. Moreover, church policy makers are wrongly blaming gay ministers for the sex abuse crisis and are contributing to destructive attitudes about homosexuality in society at large, he contends. According to Gumbleton, the real cause of sexual abuse in the church is the presence of psychologically underdeveloped priests who pursue inappropriate sexual relationships. Gay priests bring to the church unique gifts of compassion and courage and should be fully welcomed, he concludes. Gumbleton is an auxiliary bishop of the archdiocese of Detroit, Michigan.

As you read, consider the following questions:
1. According to Gumbleton, what is the message of the U.S. bishops' document, *Always Our Children?*
2. How does the author define the celibate commitment?
3. In Gumbleton's opinion, what should the Catholic Church do to prevent sexual abuse by clergy?

One major fallout of the current crisis of leadership in the Catholic Church is the scapegoating of homosexual priests and seminarians. One bishop was quoted as saying that his "unscientific conclusion is that most sexual abuse by priests is against adolescent boys and therefore is rooted in societal acceptance of homosexuality." He went on to draw the bizarre conclusion that there are some fields that should not be open to certain people: "I don't think drug addicts should be pharmacists, I don't think alcoholics should be bartenders, I don't think kleptomaniacs should be bank tellers and I don't think homosexuals should be priests." Obviously he believes every homosexual person is a sex addict and, if we barred them from the priesthood, the sex scandal would be quietly ended.

Critics of Gay Ordination

Other bishops do not go so far as to consider all homosexual men to be sex addicts; nevertheless, they bar them from the seminary and the priesthood. Their policy reflects the judgment provided in a report prepared by the theologian Germain Grisez: "Can men with a homosexual orientation become good candidates for ordination? There are reasons to doubt it. Sexuality profoundly shapes the lives of human persons, and a homosexual orientation, albeit less bizarre than the commonly recognized paraphilias, is a grave disorder. Homosexual men no doubt can be perfectly continent, but the charism of celibacy involves more; peaceful chastity and the sublimation of sexual energy into priestly service for the kingdom's sake."

Some critics of the acceptance of homosexual men into the priesthood, like Charles Wilson, head of the St. Joseph's Foundation, a canon law organization in Texas, would like to see the church make the ban on homosexual seminarians more explicit in canon law, although he contends that if canon law is interpreted correctly it already prohibits homosexual seminarians.

In fact, one bishop has already publicly taken this position. He insists: "There is a difference between a heterosexual and homosexual candidate for the priesthood. A heterosexual candidate is taking on a good thing, becoming a priest, and giving up a good thing, the desire to have a family. A gay seminarian, even a chaste one, by his orientation is not a suitable candidate for the priesthood, even if he did not commit an act of [gay sex]. He is giving up what the church considers an abomination."

[In] March [2002] Joaquin Navarro-Valls, the official spokesperson for the Vatican, publicly linked pedophile priests with homosexuality and even went so far as to suggest that gay men could not be validly ordained. His statement in itself would not be of great concern, since Dr. Navarro-Valls is not in any sense part of the church's magisterium.[1] However, his remarks seem to take on an authoritative nature, because no bishop in the Vatican or elsewhere has publicly rejected those remarks. This can certainly leave the impression that he speaks with official support.

The Scapegoating Must Stop

All of this focus on gay men in the priesthood and religious life, as a response to the recent sexual scandals, leaves many gay priests and brothers feeling very vulnerable and afraid. In a recent article one religious, Bro. Jack Talbot, a friar in the Capuchin Province of St. Joseph, quoted a friend: "It's such a difficult journey just to be out; coming out in religious life requires another level of courage and conversion. With the Vatican's recent attack on homosexuals in religious life, I fear that some parishioner will turn my orientation into something ugly and vile, and the next thing you know I will be reading about it in the local paper."

All this must stop: the scapegoating of gay priests for the sex abuse crisis, the demand to reject homosexual persons for the priesthood and religious life, the unchallenged suggestion that the ordination of a gay man would be invalid. All these positions contribute to the sharp increase in the negative feelings that so many in the church and our society have toward homosexual persons.

The first step toward reversing these harsh judgments and negative feelings about gay priests and homosexual persons

---

1. The magisterium is the teaching authority of the church, vested in the pope and in the bishops together and in union with the pope.

in general is to examine our own experience. Without being aware of it, untold numbers of people in the church have been blessed by the compassionate and healing ministry of gay priests and bishops. Ordinary common sense tells us that such ministry is of God. It is authentic and it is valid.

It might also be helpful to recall what the U.S. bishops wrote in their document *Always Our Children*. In speaking to parents who discover that their child is homosexual we asked, "How can you best express your love—itself a reflection of God's unconditional love—for your child?" And then we urged:

> Don't break off contact; don't reject your child. . . . Your child may need you and your family more than ever. He or she is still the same person. This child who has always been God's gift to you may now be the cause of another gift: your family becoming more honest, respectful and supportive. Yes, your love can be tested by this reality, but it can also grow stronger through your struggle to respond lovingly.

Would it not be a blessing for parents who are struggling to accept and unconditionally love their homosexual child if the church were to accept gay priests and bishops openly and gratefully? And if the gift of a homosexual child can be the cause of another gift to the family, is it not even more likely that a homosexual priest could be the cause of such a gift to the parish community? A community that could accept this gift would grow in its ability to be honest, respectful and supportive.

We must also ask ourselves: do we really want to deprive the church of the valuable and blessed ministry that is already being provided by priests and religious who are gay or lesbian? Do we really wish to increase the pain and hurt that many of them have experienced throughout their lives? Do we really want to instigate a "witch hunt" to expel from the ministry gay priests, and, I might add, gay bishops?

The Struggle of Gay Priests

As a bishop for over 30 years, I have worked with and come to know well many gay priests. They are healthy psychologically, and their committed ministry has been very effective. I am inspired by their love of God and of the people they serve so well and generously. I also know the struggle they now face as they see the bishops deal with the current crisis in the church.

A few letters that I have received recently show clearly how this present attack on homosexual persons is being experienced. One priest wrote:

I am a Roman Catholic priest in good standing, and celibate. I did not choose to be so, but in God's infinite love and mercy I was created a gay man. . . .

I have struggled with the knowledge of my sexuality. I have sought ways that my gifts and talents could be used fully for building the Kingdom of God. However, the fear of "witch hunts" continues to keep a part of me "in the closet." How I long to be able to be "out" (in appropriate ways) and honest with the people I serve. I feel rejection by the people I try to serve in love, which causes me much pain. Sometimes I wonder if I should remain a priest. . . .

I love the work I do. I live celibacy one day at a time, and I believe that I am a good priest. But I am also saddened that I am prevented from sharing those parts of who I am, the source of my compassion and that which energizes me. . . . I find unbearable that there is so much hate that continues to be fueled by those who claim to speak for our reconciling God.

Here is another example:

I am a priest who is gay and celibate, and I have struggled all my life with the many issues associated with being born homosexual.

The Holy Spirit has obviously called many gays to the priesthood in the last few years. How do the bishops explain that? Do the bishops understand the hatred and opposition they are stirring up toward gay priests by their remarks? Do they see that, like opposition to minorities entering the priesthood years ago, their opposition to gays has no foundation in the teachings of Jesus? Bishop Gumbleton, you have encouraged gay priests to be open about their orientation. And I have been—only to be questioned now by parishioners as someone who has been ordained mistakenly. In all my years of sacraments, today was the first time a young couple in our parish asked me if the baptism of their baby would be valid—since they had heard from their parents that I was a homosexual.

It seems clear to me that these priests who have been totally faithful in following out their call to the priesthood deserve better of us. They must not be harassed and forced to live in fear and even suffer the violence that our society often directs against homosexual persons. Open support and love for gay priests and bishops would remove the sense of isolation and loneliness that many experience. This, together with the freedom to no longer "hide an important part of who I am," would greatly lessen the number of those who otherwise might fail to be faithful to their celibate commitment.

The Celibate Commitment

And I insist that we must reject any suggestion that a gay priest or bishop cannot make the same celibate commitment a heterosexual man would make. It is a very inadequate understanding of celibacy to say that, as the bishop quoted above put it, a heterosexual priest is "giving up a good thing, the desire to have a family." Celibacy is not simply a "giving up" of something. It is a positive way of loving—truly loving and being loved—but with the exclusion of sexual intimacy. Homosexual people can also love celibately and be a sign of God's love just as genuinely as heterosexuals. In *Always Our Children* the U.S. bishops taught this clearly when they stated:

> Everyone—the homosexual and the heterosexual person—is called to personal maturity and responsibility. With the help of God's grace, everyone is called to practice the virtue of chastity in relationships. Chastity means integrating one's thoughts, feelings and actions in the area of human sexuality in a way that values and respects one's own dignity and that of others.

As a heterosexual person I have had to learn how to integrate my sexuality in a healthy way in all of my loving and mutual relationships. As a celibate person, I chose to do this without full sexual intimacy. And as Professor Grisez puts it, I arrive at a point of "peaceful chastity and the sublimation of sexual energy into priestly service for the kingdom's sake."

What is true of me as a celibate heterosexual person is just as true of the celibate homosexual person. The celibate homosexual priest or bishop brings the same charism to the service of the church as the heterosexual and can achieve the same "peaceful chastity and sublimation of sexual energy" for priestly service.

To say that the only thing a gay priest has to give up is "an abomination" manifests not only profound ignorance of what celibacy really is, but also is an insult to every homosexual person. Again, while celibacy represents a sacrifice, it is not simply a "giving up." It is a unique way of loving, a charism given by God to persons who are homosexual or heterosexual. For this reason, it is absurd to suggest that the ordination of homosexual persons is invalid simply because of their sexual orientation. Obviously God has called many gay men to the priesthood and to the episcopate throughout the whole history of the church. Indeed, to declare all of these ordinations invalid would call into question the integrity of our whole sacramental system.

The Real Cause of Sexual Abuse

Another important reason to reject this attack against homosexual priests and bishops is that by identifying homosexuals as the cause, or an important part of the cause, of the current crisis we will fail to deal with the most basic cause of the scandalous situation. The radical cause was identified in 1971 in the psychological study of Catholic priests and bishops in the United States, authored by Dr. Eugene Kennedy. This study, of course, included homosexual and heterosexual priests. It indicated that a very large percentage of priests were seriously underdeveloped in terms of psychological maturity. This can result in a situation in which a person may be chronologically an adult but psychologically, affectively and emotionally still a teenager. Obviously such persons will tend toward inappropriate relationships. (A person who is psychologically an adolescent would feel more comfortable in relationships with younger people—with "teenagers" like himself.) And whether such a relationship is homosexual or heterosexual, it is wrong and can even be criminal.

But the problem confronting us is not a problem of homosexual priests among us. It is a problem of seriously underdeveloped priests. Yet this is a problem that can be overcome. Underdeveloped persons can be guided toward a fuller stage of maturity that will enable them to function in a psychologically healthy way. This is just as true of the underdeveloped homosexual person as it is of the underdeveloped heterosexual person. The important thing to work toward in the seminary and in religious formation is approving for ordination only those persons who have achieved an adequate degree of healthy psychological development. This must include healthy psychological development for both homosexual and heterosexual persons. Various psychological studies indicate homosexual persons are as healthy as anyone else. This can also be the case among priests and bishops.

Breen. © 2002 by Copley News Service. Reproduced by permission.

There are a number of additional reasons why we must reject attacks upon homosexual priests and value their ministry in the church. For example, in his book, *Spiritual Direction and the Gay Person*, James Empereur, S.J., states: "Homosexuality is one of God's most significant gifts to humanity. Through their testimony of suffering, God has chosen gays and lesbians to reveal something about God that heterosexuals do not." Drawing on this insight, Bro. Jack Talbot points out that homosexuals "minister through the language of our pain, of our passion story. As we begin a new century, a recontextualized gospel of reconciliation is required, and healing medicine can be offered from the marginalized. Our gay and lesbian brothers and sisters can help our institution during this moment of suffering and humiliation."

I agree. What a loss if we drive these "gifted" people from our midst!

God's Healing Balm

A further gift gay priests bring to our church is an exceptional ability and courage to proclaim the truth—something demanded by the prophetic nature of the priesthood. This can happen because of the often arduous "coming out" process homosexuals must undertake. Gay and lesbian people have had to identify, accept and affirm a truth about themselves that others have defamed. Coming to this awareness can be enormously difficult. In fact, it often had to be done without any encouragement or guideposts from others. They have often experienced opposition to knowing the truth about themselves, accepting their truth, and being willing even to share it with others. By living out this painful process, gay priests develop a deeply prophetic courage.

Gay priests also can offer a depth of compassion not always shared in a comparable way by heterosexual priests. Gay people have often been treated as outcasts by society, church and even family. Because of this experience, they can develop an awareness and sensitivity to those who are being excluded and included in various situations. Such a gift of compassion surely enriches one who is called to minister to others.

For all of these reasons, I urge our church leadership to rejoice in the blessings that can come to us by recognizing and supporting gay priests rather than shunning or rejecting them. Bro. Jack Talbot describes very well what needs to happen if we hope to achieve a good resolution of the current crisis in the church:

> The church hierarchy needs to accept the help of her gay and lesbian members as ministers of healing, rather than making us scapegoats for a problem that we did nothing to create. Let us be advocates for the church during this crisis. Hear our stories. . . . For many, our gay and lesbian brothers and sisters may be unlikely teachers. Nevertheless, they can be God's healing balm, God's grace and peace at a time when the fragility of our society is painfully demonstrated in the crisis spots that are in the forefront of the news and in the frailty of the human heart.

"The celibacy requirement [is] part of the cause of clergy abuse of children."

The Celibacy Requirement for Priests Fosters Child Sexual Abuse

Sarah McCarthy

The sexually repressive demands of the Catholic Church, particularly the celibacy requirement for priests, have contributed to the crisis of child sexual abuse by clergy, writes Sarah McCarthy in the following viewpoint. When the natural sex drive is suppressed, it often finds destructive outlets, resulting in an excessive preoccupation with sex, a distorted sexual identity, and pedophilia, the author contends. She maintains that the church could curb future sexual abuse by eliminating the priestly celibacy requirement and by ordaining women. McCarthy, a freelance writer, is coauthor of *Mom and Pop vs. the Dreambusters.*

As you read, consider the following questions:
1. For what reasons would the Catholic Church consider nearly all of its members to be "sexual sinners," according to McCarthy?
2. According to John Money, quoted by the author, what are the effects of sexually repressive environments on girls and boys?
3. Why does McCarthy think that sexual abuse victims should pursue quiet settlements and counseling rather than widely publicized lawsuits?

Sarah McCarthy, "Behind the Vestry Door," *Liberty*, vol. 16, June 2002, pp. 21–24. Copyright © 2002 by the Liberty Foundation. Reproduced by permission.

A funeral Mass was held April 7 [2002], for the Rev. Dan Rooney, 48, a Roman Catholic priest who was found recently slumped over the wheel of his car with a gunshot wound to the head, three days after he was accused of molesting a young girl two decades ago. The suicide of Father Rooney, and the disappearance of Chandra Levy, connected perhaps, it they are connected at all, only by tenuous links of inferred sexual shame—the kind of deep sexual shame and fear that can result in death—one by suicide, the other a possible homicide by a man terrified at the threatened exposure of his sexual secrets, remind us that sexual outings are by their nature infused with danger.[1]

In a nation that has become habituated to sexual spectacles, the current scandal within the Church is particularly tragic because of the tender age of the victims and the homosexuality of many of the priests, compounded by the Church's tempestuousness regarding sexual matters and the higher sensitivity to shame and guilt possessed by men of the cloth. . . .

The Culture of the Church

The priest scandal raises questions about the culture of the Roman Catholic Church that is shaping and maintaining the behavior of its priests. Though I am a flown away Catholic and have not been immersed in the subterraneanly tempestuous culture of the Church since the age of 22, I have been thinking lately about the Church's culture. Perhaps it was the timing, since I had just emerged from adolescence and was entering early adulthood when I left, but the salient culture of the Church I remember was a cloyingly anxiety-producing mix of sexual repression, whispered guilt, and shame over small sins, followed by the relief of the confessional. At baptisms, devils are cast out and "unclean mothers" are forbidden to approach the altar. Like a government with ubiquitous regulations, most Catholics of child-bearing age live in widespread noncompliance with the sexual laws of the Church, making sexual sinners out of nearly all the

---

1. Washington, D.C., intern Chandra Levy was murdered in 2001. California representative Gary Condit, who had been romantically involved with Levy, was widely suspected of being linked to her murder but was never charged.

members. The sexual requirements—abstinence, celibacy, prohibition of birth control, and the intolerance of homosexuality and divorce are not only unreasonable, but not even desirable as ideals.

Biological determinism and the behaviorism of psychologists like Skinner are currently out of vogue, overshadowed in favor of personal responsibility as the exclusive politically correct determinant of behavior; but there is nothing so personally irresponsible as the wholesale denial by institutions like the Church of biological and cultural realities. All people have sex drives put there by nature, and damming them up, as opposed to rationally managing them, results in bizarre outcomes just as a dammed up river will overflow its banks and wreak havoc.

Sexual Repression and Pedophilia

In fact, statements by Dr. Jay Feierman, a psychiatrist who has seen hundreds of pedophile priests at a Catholic treatment center for abusive priests in New Mexico, support a link between sexual repression and pedophilia. Feierman says that celibacy is not "a natural state for humans to be in." Pointing to the celibacy requirement as being part of the cause of clergy abuse of children, he explains: "If you tell a man that he's not allowed to have particular friends, he's not allowed to be affectionate, he's not allowed to be in love, he's not allowed to be a sexual being, you shouldn't be surprised at anything that happens."

Research by the University of New Hampshire's David Finkelhor, Ph.D., supports those observations. Finkelhor, a recognized expert on the study of sexual abuse of children, has shown that repressive sexual attitudes linked to many religions may predispose some persons toward sexual activities with children, and Dr. John Money, a leading expert on sexual violence who has pioneered treatments for deviate sexuality at Johns Hopkins Medical School, adds that people raised in conditions where sex is viewed as evil, and where sexual curiosity is considered a punishable offense, are likely to end up with warped sexual identities.

Money describes the harmful effects of such environments as follows: "In girls, often you extinguish the lust completely, so that they can never have an orgasm, and marriage becomes a dreary business where you put up with sex to serve the maternal instinct. In boys, sex gets redirected into abnormal channels."

This is not new information. Five centuries ago, Martin Luther observed that the Catholic Church's leaders "were completely unjustified in forbidding marriage and in burdening the priesthood with the demand of continual celibacy. In doing so they have acted like . . . tyrannical, unholy scoundrels, occasioning all sorts of terrible, ghastly, countless sins against chastity, in which they are caught to this day."

Medieval Denial

The Church remains in medieval denial about the reality of the sex drive—its dogma allowing for no compromise or alternative outlets—not masturbation or birth control to avoid pregnancy, not married priests to avoid "burning," as Saint Paul would put it, and certainly not adult homosexual sex. Like a naive teenager afraid to plan ahead for possible sexual occurrences that could result in unplanned pregnancies and abortions, the Church's stubborn state of denial gives rise to unpredictable and destructive eruptions. Just as a fasting person or a dieter becomes obsessed with food, and is likely to binge on junk food, young celibates become inordinately preoccupied with sex. With such a damming up of the sex drive, heaven only knows where it will find outlets. Just as male heterosexuals denied sex in prison engage in homosexual behavior, and members of the Taliban forbidden the temptation of looking at or associating with women engage in sex with each other, celibacy might result in even children and sheep beginning to look like viable sex partners.[2] As Francis Bacon put it, nature to be commanded must be obeyed.

The imposition of impossible edicts makes spiritual liars out of people, causing worse behaviors than the ones Church authorities try to eliminate. At the end of the day, I suspect it will be recognized that the fatal flaw in the Church is not sexual license brought on by the '60s, or the acceptance of

2. The Taliban was an Islamic fundamentalist sect that ruled Afghanistan from 1996 to 2001.

gays in the seminary, but its overwhelming sexual repression, the same sort of repression that has led to the nutty displacement behaviors seen in radical Islamic cultures.

For gays to become the scapegoats of the priest mess would be a mistake. It would only add more insult and injury to gays, without addressing the Church's root problem—sexual repression. Historically and internationally, heterosexual child abuse has been a frequent occurrence in the Church.

The Spirit of Forbidden Sex

It is interesting to speculate about why gays are so heavily involved in the priest mess, and how their behavior might be shaped by Church culture. If you're gay and out of place in the mainstream couples culture, life in an all-male, non-married hierarchy where heterosexual couples and women are banished feels comfortable and safe. Incredibly, the Catholic Church might be inadvertently running the biggest closet in town. The atmosphere of steamy repressed sex, guilt, secret confession, repentance, relief, and forgiveness might not only provide shelter, but might just get sexy after awhile, like the priests many remember from their Catholic adolescence, who were a little too interested, with a ear close to adolescent confessions.

The Catholic Church has a dread of sex that is second only perhaps to Islam. This is a Church that explains away the sex linkage to births by proclaiming that they were achieved by virgins. When I was a young girl, virginity was about the only ticket to sainthood. Saint Maria Goretti was extolled for permitting a man to stab her rather than submit to rape. The mother of God was a virgin, and the subtitle of our parish was "the church of the sorrowful virgin." Eve, who had brought down mankind, was a temptress. Lesbians and gays simply didn't exist, and nuns went to town in pairs of two, covered in garb not unlike the burqas of Islam. The spirit of incipient, subterranean forbidden sex was everywhere. Kids giggled at the sight of a wisp of graying blond hair fringing out of Sister Pierre's veil. Believe me, we are better off shocked at the sight of Britney Spears' breasts than Sister Pierre's stray hair clump. I remember an eighth-grade classmate being slapped in the face by a nun in the front of the class for wearing a light natural lipstick, and the nuns forbidding patent leather shoes because they reflected upwards. Though Americans consider themselves to be sophisticated, enlightened, and modern, it's not been that long since American Catholics were subjected to the kind of environment found under the Islamic Commission for the Promotion of Virtue and the Prevention of Vice.

The Problem with Hardball Tactics

A recent poll by *USA Today* reports that eleven percent of Roman Catholics have personal knowledge of sex abuse by priests, and according to Gallup, 72% of Catholics believe the problem is widespread. For the most part, victims and their families have decided to deal with the problem privately rather than casting themselves as victims, with all that entails, in the center ring of a sex abuse scandal. Before the Church's quiet handling of the scandals is turned into a scorch and burn frenzy, it's important to remember that if victims and their families had not wanted it brushed under the rug, it never would have been.

Richard Cage, who has investigated pedophile cases for

the police in Montgomery County, Md., for 25 years, says that "Our biggest challenge is when it involves the Church. Denial is our biggest problem. Parents are reluctant to have their child interviewed. And of the children that have been abused, at first 99% will deny it."

And who can blame the victim for not wanting to come forward? What child and his or her family want to embark in a mud slinging contest with the Catholic Church and with their friends and neighbors and relatives who refuse to believe that the parish priest whom they love and admire could be guilty of such a thing? Which child wants to cast himself as the pariah and joke of the neighborhood?

Opting under political pressures for a cure that will probably be worse than the disease, [in the spring of 2002] the New York Archdiocese said it would drop its policy of not reporting alleged child sexual abuse to police. Cardinal Egan says that if there is reasonable cause to believe an allegation, and if the victim does not object, civil authorities will be notified. Egan's statement fell flat with critics, write reporters Douglas Montero and Dan Mangan in the *New York Post:*

> "Talk is cheap," said David Clohessy, national director of Survivors Network of Those Abused by Priests. "Few Catholic leaders have been as insensitive to abuse victims as Egan has. He's full of hollow-sounding pronouncements, but the evidence clearly shows that he has impugned the motives of abuse survivors, and used hardball legal tactics time and again, and treated people who were hurting like the enemy."
> Also yesterday, Manhattan DA Robert Morgenthau said he has told a lawyer for the archdiocese he would seek to extend the state's mandatory reporting law to include priests.

In his anger and outrage, David Clohessy of the Survivor's Network has inadvertently embarked on a strategy ensuring that even more abused people will have hardball legal tactics used against them. Some of the accused will be innocent, others will be terrified and will hire tough lawyers. In war and in lawsuits, truth is the first casualty. Victim groups never seem to understand that once they bring their grievances to the legal arena, such tactics are inevitable. Considering the alternatives, the methods the Church has been using to handle these problems—privacy, counseling, and settlements—do not look so bad.

Curbing Future Pedophilia

Rather than resorting to a punitive purge of priests, with a cast of characters that inevitably will include false and real perpetrators, truthful and delusional accusers, ecclesiastical versions of the coffee spill lady, and the inevitable suicides, the Church should find the courage to focus on curbing future pedophilia by widening the group from which priests are chosen to include women and by eliminating celibacy requirements. Columnists Maureen Dowd and Andrew Sullivan have suggested that to limit abuse by priests, women must be brought into the Church hierarchy. Dowd writes in the *New York Times* that:

> A monsoon of sickening stories lately illustrate how twisted societies become when women are either never seen, dismissed as second-class citizens or occluded by testosterone: the church subsidizing pedophilia; the Afghan warlords' resumption of pedophilia; the Taliban obliteration of women; . . . the repression of women, even American servicewomen, by our allies the Saudis.

> The Saudi religious police let 15 little girls die in a school blaze in Mecca. The police—the Commission for the Promotion of Virtue and Prevention of Vice—stopped men who tried to rescue the girls or open the school gates, telling them "it is sinful to approach" the girls because they weren't wearing head scarves and abayas, and there could be no exposure of "females to male strangers.". . . the Saudi police were operating on the philosophy "Better a dead girl than a bareheaded girl."

Dowd is right, of course, that the obliteration of women results in twisted societies, but she's missing the point that the obliteration of women is really just the symptom of an insidious underlying problem—pathological sexual repression. Sexual repression underlies each of the aforementioned sickening stories. . . . The inclusion of women in societies, is, in itself, no guarantee that things will not become twisted. Feminists have enabled American women to gain access to the workplace, but the excessive punitiveness of sexual harassment lawsuits, or the threat of sexual harassment lawsuits, is a sexually repressive process that itself ensures twisted stories, endlessly spotlighting legal-political sexual scandals, and maybe even some deaths like Chandra Levy's.

Feminists have embarked on a purification drive in the workplace not unlike the Saudi policy of "better dead than bareheaded," that instead, inadvertently becomes "better dead than sexually harassed." High stakes legal shamefests casting women as victim whistle-blowers that ruin families, workplaces, and careers, is a twisted strategy that sends unprepared women to play with fire. . . .

Respecting Victims' Rights

If victims don't want to come forward and star in a legal-political circus, their rights should be respected. If they choose the dignity of quiet settlements and counseling, that should be their prerogative. Despite the widespread hysteria about the exploitation of an intern by the president of the United States, ask Monica Lewinsky, now or in 20 years, who abused her—Bill Clinton or the American legal-political system that outed her in the wake of the Paula Jones sexual harassment case, and the sanctimonious American media.[3]

Americans should reconsider whether or not the legal system is the best first choice venue for solving sexual issues. Most Catholics know the terror of confessing private sins to a priest in a dark booth. Imagine the terror of sexual sins being heralded across the front page. It is the political equivalent of a public execution. As the moralists like to tell us, sunlight is the best disinfectant. But sunlight also brings drought, and burns, parches, and kills shade-loving plants. Draconian mandatory legal processes may, in fact, make victims, either young teens or their families, even less likely to come forward to complain about an errant priest.

3. In 1998 President Bill Clinton admitted that he had had an affair with White House intern Monica Lewinsky.

"There is no evidence that the rate [of sexual abuse] for [Catholic] priests is higher than that for any other non-celibate group."

The Celibacy Requirement for Priests Does Not Foster Child Sexual Abuse

Philip Jenkins

In the following viewpoint Philip Jenkins maintains that there is no link between mandatory priestly celibacy and the sexual abuse of minors. Moreover, Jenkins notes, most people are misinformed about the nature of celibacy in the Catholic priesthood. Priestly celibacy arose in the early church, which believed that celibate priests would focus more on spiritual rather than worldly concerns. Celibacy is also recognized as a means to transform sexual energy into a source of strength —an attitude that reflects a deep respect for the power of sexuality rather than contempt for it, the author explains. While the church may eventually reconsider its policy on mandatory celibacy, there is no evidence that abandoning celibacy would prevent child sexual abuse. Jenkins is a professor of history and religious studies at Pennsylvania State University and the author of *Pedophiles and Priests*.

As you read, consider the following questions:
1. What are the most common misunderstandings about the history of priestly celibacy, in Jenkins's opinion?
2. According to the author, what change in church ritual brought about the demand for permanent priestly celibacy?

In March [2002], as cases of sexual abuse by Catholic clergy have appeared regularly in the headlines, the notion of priestly celibacy has become the subject of talk radio and dinner party discussions. But much of the debate has been rooted in myth and misinformation and clouded by the assumption, particularly in this country, that the time has come for the Roman Catholic Church to end this Medieval foolishness and do away with the practice. In fact, the subject is much more complex. And barring unforeseen circumstances, celibacy is likely to be around in the American Catholic church for a long time to come.

The popular view seems to be that celibacy reflects a hatred and contempt for sexuality—and for women—and that it turns priests into frustrated loners who express their inner conflicts through sexual assaults on little children. For many reasons, I think these charges are unfair.

I belong to a church that does not require celibacy of its clergy and has female priests, namely the Episcopal Church. Yet speaking as a historian, I can understand the reasons another church might require priestly celibacy. And as a consumer of news, I see that celibacy's origins and the church's motivations in requiring it are widely misunderstood.

The Origins of Priestly Celibacy

Let's start with what has become a standard misstatement about its genesis: That priests were required to be celibate beginning around 1100, maybe even a little later. We do know that compulsory celibacy was not a practice of the earliest church. We know that Saint Peter had a mother-in-law, that the apostles traveled in the company of their wives, and that some early popes were (without causing scandal) the sons of other popes. Yet beyond these facts, much is in doubt.

The notion that mandatory celibacy wasn't imposed until the 12th century, stated as "fact," seems quite damning to the church's insistence on the practice. If true, modern Catholics would be insisting on an innovation that has been around for less than half of the history of Christianity, one that dates to the Middle Ages, a period that enjoys a dreadful reputation in modern thought. Through guilt by association, celibacy seems to be linked in many people's minds with such horrors as witch-burning, the Inquisition and the Crusades. Worst of all, the reasons often cited for the invention of celibacy are not even spiritual, but rather involve land rights. According to a scholarly myth widely held among historians, the church was just trying to ensure that the children of priests could not become legitimate heirs to church land. Literally, according to this story, the modern Catholic Church is keeping alive a survival of feudal times.

This pseudo-history is wrong at almost every point. Mandatory celibacy goes much further back than Medieval times, if not quite to the days of the apostles. Priestly celibacy was the usual expectation in the West by late Roman times, say the 4th century, and Medieval statements on the subject were just reasserting discipline that had collapsed temporarily in times of war and social chaos. Of course we can find married priests throughout the Middle Ages, just as we can find priests committing molestation today, but that does not mean that, in either case, they were acting with church approval.

In making this point about dates, I am not just nitpicking in the worst academic tradition. I am stressing that priestly celibacy is a product of the very early church. Just how early? It was celibate priests and monks who made the final decisions about which books were going to make up the New Testament, and which would be excluded. If, as most Christians believe, the ideas and practices of the early church carry special authority, then we should certainly rank priestly celibacy among these ancient traditions.

Celibacy as a Source of Strength

So if they were not defending land rights, why did successive popes try to enforce celibacy? Odd as this may seem, the main reason seems to have been the increased frequency of the Eucharist or Mass. Because of the need to focus on spiritual rather than worldly interests, married priests in the 3rd and 4th centuries were supposed to abstain from sex the night before saying Mass. As Mass became a daily ritual, this effectively demanded permanent celibacy. Out of this practical need came a whole theology of self-sacrifice. The idea of celibacy is based less on a fear of sexuality than on a deep respect for its power, and with proper training, a celibate could transform or channel this power into a source of strength. Modern psychologists would later invent the term "sublimation" for this complex process.

Making True Love Possible

When I decided to go into the seminary at the age of 28, I broke up with my girlfriend—not because I was suddenly opposed to marriage, but because church law requires it. Asked whether I would have chosen a life of celibacy had it not been required, I have to admit that I would not have. But I experienced a profound call to follow without reservations or conditions, and in that spirit, I accepted the celibacy requirement with trepidation, but with the faith that I would be sustained in doing whatever it took to conform to it. Throughout the years, though, I have come to value the vow of celibacy highly. . . .

Celibacy has more to do with poverty than with sex. It is the radical, outward expression of the poverty of the human heart, the poverty that makes true love possible by preventing it from corrupting into possession or manipulation. That is why child abuse by priests is so shocking, so horrible, so destructive. It places celibacy at the service of power and lust, not of love.

Lorenzo Albacete, *New York Times Magazine*, March 31, 2002.

By giving up the most basic human needs and comforts, the priest was able to devote himself entirely to God and to the people he served. He was meant to treat all the faithful equally, with no need to give special preference to a wife or children. A "father" was meant to be father to all. Of course, changes in society mean that the church no longer needs to prove that its clergy stand above the narrow ties of kin, but other reasons for celibacy remain unchanged. In some ways, the case for celibacy may even be greater today than it was centuries ago. In a society that seems to be so thoroughly aware of sex and sexuality, maybe even obsessed with it, what greater self-sacrifice could there be, what greater rejection of the culture, than the adoption of celibacy?

At the same time, not even the Catholic Church claims that clerical celibacy is a strict matter of faith that can never be changed. The church indeed says that some of its teachings can never be softened—for instance, the prohibition on female priests or the ban on abortion. But it also makes clear that celibacy (like matters of liturgical practice, for example) is a question of internal church discipline, which could be changed if circumstances demanded it. Such a change would not require any embarrassing backtracking on past policies, any kind of reversal of once "infallible" statements.

It may come as a surprise that Catholic authorities do allow a little flexibility in the matter of married priests. If, for instance, a priest converts to Catholicism from a church that allows marriage, like the Orthodox, then he may be able to enter the Roman church as a married priest in good standing. Some have done so—often to the annoyance of mainstream Catholic clergy, who are not granted this same privilege.

Should the Church Change Its Stand?

But now let me ask an outrageous question: Why *should* the Roman Catholic Church change its stance on celibacy? Much has been said of late about the damage that celibacy inflicts on the modern church and its poor exploited believers. But, like the pseudo-history, many of these contemporary charges are false.

Among the harms caused by celibacy, two possibilities come to mind. One, obviously, is the problem of "pedophile priests," who allegedly commit their crimes because of the frustration and immaturity caused directly by celibacy. The reform motto is beautiful in its simplicity, and inspiring in its urgency: End celibacy and save the children! Yet there is no credible evidence to link the two. Many of the same problems also happen in churches and denominations that allow clergy to marry. Based on some excellent studies using large samples of priests, we can say that about 2 or 3 percent of Catholic priests are sexually involved with minors. There is no evidence that the rate for these priests is higher than that for any other non-celibate group. So how does celibacy come into the picture at all?

Another issue more plausibly connected with celibacy is the growth of gay subcultures in the American priesthood—not that having homosexual priests is necessarily bad in itself. But when men with gay inclinations are represented in the priesthood at a rate 10 or 20 times that in the average male population (which studies suggest is the case), this does tend to make the priesthood more of a closed caste separated from the lives of ordinary believers. But ending celibacy now almost certainly would not change the situation, or make the priesthood less gay. Just look at my own Episcopal church, in which clergy have been allowed to marry since the 16th century: The Episcopal clergy has flourishing gay subcultures quite as active as those rumored in the Roman church, only far more public.

Two Possibilities

Ultimately, the Catholic stance on priestly celibacy can change in one of two ways, neither of which seems very likely. The American church could go into schism, declaring its independence from Rome, which nobody is predicting. The only alternative is to wait for Rome and the global church to declare changes from the center, an idea that reformers have prayed for over the years. As the hopeful joke goes, at the Third Vatican Council, the pope will bring his wife; at the Fourth Vatican Council, the pope will bring her husband. Yet today, the chances for that sort of reform seem bleak.

There are any number of reasons the Roman Catholic Church might want to end mandatory celibacy for its clergy. It might rethink the theology of the whole matter; it might carry out surveys showing that a married priesthood would simply do a better pastoral job of ministering to the faithful. Above all, it might decide that ending celibacy is simply the only way to restore the numbers of the priesthood, and that seems to me an excellent idea—though as I say, I write as an outsider. But whatever it does, let the church decide its course on celibacy for the right reasons. Let it act according to the logic of its own principles, and not in response to bogus history and convenient mythology.

"['A culture of dissent'] created within the
Church an invisible schism . . . first inside
the minds, the hearts and the souls of
individuals and later in the institution of
the Church itself."

A Culture of Dissent Contributes to Child Sexual Abuse

George Weigel

In the following viewpoint George Weigel argues that the Catholic Church's sex abuse crisis is rooted in what he refers to as a "culture of dissent." This culture of dissent, which developed over the past four decades, includes a rejection of traditional church teachings on birth control, homosexuality, and celibacy, Weigel maintains. He contends that while many priests publicly agree with official church policies, they inwardly reject them and refuse to preach about them in their parishes. Thus, Weigel writes, many clergy have led self-deceptive double lives, corrupting the institutional church and creating an unhealthy environment in which immorality can flourish. Weigel, a theologian, is the author of *The Courage to Be Catholic*.

As you read, consider the following questions:

1. According to Weigel, what are the five main misperceptions concerning the sex abuse crisis in the Catholic Church?
2. In the author's opinion, why was the Catholic Church's "culture of dissent" allowed to prevail?

George Weigel, "The Courage to Be Catholic," speech on March 22, 2003, Chicago/Oakbrook CMF Conference. Reproduced by permission of the author.

The first thing to understand for a genuine Catholic reform in the Church in America is that the clergy sex scandal is a crisis of priestly identity. Priests who genuinely believe themselves to be what the Catholic Church teaches they are, namely, icons living representations of the eternal Priesthood of Jesus Christ simply do not behave as sexual predators. Priests who believe themselves to be deeply internalized, that sense of themselves as icons of the eternal Priesthood of Jesus Christ, simply do not behave as sexual predators.

Secondly, it is a crisis of leadership of the Bishops of the United States; a scandal of clergy sexual malfeasance was turned into a crisis because of the failure of Bishops to lead. That failure reflects a crisis in episcopal identity. Bishops who believe themselves to be what the Church teaches they are: namely, successors of the Apostles, successors of Peter, Andrew, Paul, James and John and all the rest do not respond to scandal as crisis managers, they respond to scandal as Apostles.

But in the third place it is very important to recognize that this is a crisis of discipleship. And that means it involves all of us. Every crisis in the history of the Church from the flight of the Apostles on Holy Thursday night to today, is caused by a deficiency of sanctity and conviction in the Church. And that is all of our business.

This crisis of fidelity can only be addressed by a deeper fidelity on the part of all the people of the Church. So when I title my book *The Courage To Be Catholic* that is what I am talking about: the courage to live ever more authentic, indeed radically Catholic lives of vocational commitment. That is everybody's task in the Church because out of that will come the Saints who will renew and reform the Church, as it has been Saints who have renewed and reformed the Church for the past 2,000 years.

A Misunderstood Crisis

It is just as important to understand what the crisis is *not* as it is to understand what the crisis is. First of all, this is not a crisis caused by celibacy. At the most elementary level and on the scandal side of the equation, it seems clear that this is a crisis caused by men failing to honor the celibate commitments they had made to Christ in the Church. To blame this crisis on celibacy is something like blaming treason on the Pledge of Allegiance. When a man commits treason, we don't say "Gee, there must be something wrong with the Pledge of Allegiance, maybe we should go back and rewrite the Pledge of Allegiance". No, we say the man has committed treason; because naming the deed accurately is the only way to address it properly.

The Problem with Liberal Clergy

Some portion of the Catholic and liberal Protestant church memberships are members because of their clergy's advocacy of liberal views that they share. Many a Catholic parish has a popular and active "Social Justice Committee," which can safely be assumed not to be concerned about the problems of small landlords squeezed by rent control but rather to be promoting the usual liberal agenda . . .

It is not my intention to argue that the clergy of the mainstream Protestant and Catholic churches of the United States are predominantly pacifists, socialists, bleeding hearts, wimps and/or indifferent to Scripture and their churches' official doctrines. But it needs to be kept in mind that such clerics are indeed plentiful. Ordained status does not guarantee accuracy even as to basic church teachings, and when church leaders make pronouncements on subjects far afield . . . great skepticism as to the basis in religion is appropriate.

M. Lester O'Shea, *St. Croix Review*, August 2003.

It is also self-evidently absurd to suggest that this crisis would not have happened if the Catholic Church, in its Latin rite, had married clergy. This is absurd because other Christian Communions in the United States have problems of clergy sexual malfeasance that are according to some studies greater than those in the Catholic Church. So a married clergy is no barrier in those institutions to these problems. But at a deeper theological level, to suggest that this crisis would not have happened had the discipline of celibacy been relaxed or removed in the Latin Rite Church is to turn marriage into a crime prevention program. And those of us who are married rather resent the thought. Marriage, as understood from a Catholic theological perspective, is a covenant of self-giving love, receptivity and fruitfulness. It is not a crime prevention program, so Father [Richard] McBrien and all the others should stop telling us that most of the Church is in a crime prevention program and that is the answer to the whole thing.

Secondly, it is not the case that this crisis has been caused by "authoritarianism" in the Church. In fact, on the episcopal leadership side of the equation, it is manifestly a failure to use the legitimate authority conferred by the Sacrament of Episcopal Ordination in Communion with the Holy See that has led a scandal into being a crisis. But at a deeper level, this cannot be a crisis caused by authoritarianism because the Catholic Church is not an authoritarian institution. The Catholic Church is a Communion of Disciples formed by an authoritative tradition and it is that tradition which forms the Church and gives it its form without reference to which there can be no reform. But that is not authoritarianism. Authoritarianism is "you do what I say because I say it". That's not the way the Church works. The Church is a Communion of Disciples gathered by an authoritative tradition answerable to that tradition. The Church is not something we make up. The Church is something whose form is given to us by Christ and there can be no reform of the Church that is authentically Catholic without reference to that form.

The Dominant Form of Abuse

Third, the tag "Pedophilia Crisis" quickly got attached to this in January 2002 because of the Geoghan case in Boston. What we know fifteen months later empirically is that pedophilia, in the strict sense of the term, namely the sexual abuse of prepubescent minors, is not in any way, shape or form the dominant form of sexual abuse that has come to light in the past fifteen months. It is the most disgusting and revolting form of abuse, but it is not the dominant form. The dominant form of abuse seems to be the homosexual abuse of teenage boys and young men often in school or seminary. This raises a whole set of issues that simply have to be addressed in a more forthright way.

Fourth, I think it is very important for faithful Catholic people who are inclined to view this as a crisis created by an anti-Catholic media, must recognize that this is not the case. It is certainly true that those elements of the national press that are deeply set against the Church, primarily because of the Church's Pro-Life witness and the Church's resistance to an unfettered biotechnology revolution and the redefinition of marriage, etc. have seen their opportunities and have taken them. We must recognize that this is not the media's crisis, this is the Church's crisis.

Finally, it is not the case, as the Catholic left wants to say, caused by the Catholic sexual ethic. This is a crisis caused by a failure to understand, internalize and live the Church's sexual ethic. It is a crisis caused in part by a failure to understand, to believe and to teach that the Catholic Church has a higher, nobler, more deeply humanistic view of human sexuality than the editors of *Playboy* and *Cosmopolitan*. And the failure to take that truth into the world and teach it has helped create the swamp of American culture today out of which these problems emerged.

What Happened?

Now, how did this all happen? It is a long and complicated story. I tried to unravel some of the threads in my book *The Courage To Be Catholic*. Perhaps I can sum up my proposal by saying that it helps to think about these problems through the prism of environmentalism of all things, and to think about these problems both in terms of scandal and in terms of the failure of leadership by Bishops. Also in terms of a damaged Catholic ecology, a damaged Catholic environment, a damaged ecclesial environment over the past 35 years, which like all damaged ecologies, eventually produce diseases, mutations and in this case, forms of spiritual death.

The crucial factor in the damaged Catholic ecology of the past decades has been what I call in the book "a culture of dissent". It created within the Church an invisible schism and an invisible fracture in the Communion of the Church, first inside the minds, the hearts and the souls of individuals and later in the institution of the Church itself. There is no reckoning with that invisible schism, that culture of dissent, that does not take account of what I call the "truths of 1968" when overt dissent by clergy, theologians, religious and even some Bishops from the authoritative teaching of Paul VI in the encyclical *Humanae Vitae* was allowed to prevail. It was allowed to prevail because some feared that a direct confrontation with dissent would create a schism in the Church, a fracture in the Church.

An Invisible Fracture

Well, we did not have a public fracture in the Church, but we did have an invisible schism, an invisible fracture in which, for example, in seminaries over some twenty years, men learned to live essentially double lives. With lives of intellectual and spiritual deception, they would pay formal *public* agreement to the teaching of the Church on the proper means of regulating families, on homosexuality, on celibacy, and on the ordination of women to the priesthood. They would make a public agreement to that, but in their minds and hearts they did not believe and accept those things, had no intention of defending them in their ministry, no intention of preaching them in their work as teachers, and thus led lives of self-deception intellectually and spiritually. This had a tremendously corrupting effect on the lives of seminarians, the lives of priests and frankly, on the lives of Bishops.

It is not implausible to suggest that men who have become accustomed to living lives of intellectual self-deception then become accustomed too readily to leading lives of behavioral self-deception as well.

The Holy Father said much the same thing [in] April 2002 when in an address to the Cardinals of the United States, summoned to Rome to sort some of this out, the Pope said that this crisis at the bottom line resulted from a failure to live and to teach "the fullness of Catholic faith". If we are not living and teaching the fullness of Catholic faith, the Church is going to become corrupt as indeed it has done at many previous moments in its earlier history.

Men and women of the culture of dissent are brothers and sisters in Christ. They deserve our prayers. But it seems to me that no good is served by denying the realities of the invisible schism in the Church. We must think carefully and concretely about how that is going to be addressed at all levels. In elementary education, secondary education, and particularly in Catholic colleges and universities it is essential that some Bishops somewhere have the courage to get up and say "I am sorry to have to say this, but in my judgment "x" can no longer be considered a Catholic college or university.

Hope Versus Optimism

The title of my biography of Pope John Paul II is *Witness to Hope* because that is how the Pope defined himself in his address to the United Nations in 1995. It is very important to distinguish hope from optimism. Optimism is a matter of optics and how things look can change from one minute to the next or from one day to the next. Hope is a theological virtue. The Pope is a witness to hope not because he is an optimist, but because he is a man of profound faith. The virtue of hope rests on the theological virtue of faith. The Pope can be a man of hope precisely because he is a man of faith. And that is the challenge embedded in this crisis for all of us to deepen our own faith so that we too can be witnesses to hope in the Church and in the world.

In the mid-1930s as the shadows of totalitarianism, which so affected the life of [Hungarian Cardinal] Joszef Mindszenty, were lengthening across Europe, Pope Pius XI wrote: "Let us thank God that He makes us live among the present problems. It is no longer permitted for anyone to be mediocre". That, I suggest, should be our watchword in transforming crisis into opportunity.

In the Bible, the Greek word "crisis" means two things. In the first instance, what we instinctively think of is a cataclysmic mess. But crisis in the Bible also means opportunity. It is a crossroad; it is an opportunity for deepening one's faith, deepening one's relationship with Christ, deepening one's relationship to the Church.

And that, it seems to me, is God's purpose in all of this. If, as Pope John Paul II said at Fatima [Portugal], on May 13, 1982, one year to the day after he was shot down in his front yard, in the designs of providence there are no mere coincidences. If that is true, then the purpose in all of this sorrow, all of this embarrassment and all of this ugliness must be to call the Church to a deeper, truer reform of itself according to the mind of the Second Vatican Council as authoritatively interpreted by this great Pope. So, let us thank God that He makes us live among these present problems. It is no longer permitted for anyone to be mediocre.

"Secrecy . . . is responsible for the depth of the current [sex abuse] crisis."

A Culture of Secrecy Contributes to Child Sexual Abuse

Larry B. Stammer

The sex abuse scandal in the Catholic Church cannot be blamed on one single issue, argues Larry B. Stammer in the following viewpoint. For example, while many experts agree that priestly celibacy in itself does not lead to sexual abuse, it can be a source of strain for emotionally immature priests. Similarly, Stammer points out, homosexuality may be a source of unhealthy stress for priests with retarded psychosexual development. He concludes, however, that this recent crisis is most deeply rooted in the church's culture of secrecy, which encouraged several Catholic bishops to knowingly hide the facts about abusive priests from the public. Stammer is a staff writer for the *Los Angeles Times*.

As you read, consider the following questions:
1. How have different constituencies in the Catholic Church responded to the sex abuse scandal, according to Stammer?
2. What kind of dilemmas do gay priests face in the Catholic Church, according to the author?
3. What kinds of accountability provisions are available to non-Catholic Christian denominations, according to Stammer?

The sexual-abuse scandal rocking the Roman Catholic Church in the U.S. has prompted calls for reforms that often blame the crisis on a single issue: Celibacy. Or homosexuality. Or secrecy. Or imperious bishops.

But what has made this scandal more intense and prolonged than its predecessors is the complex way each of these issues interlock.

The complexity explains why the scandal has outraged and energized such a wide range of church constituencies: Liberal Catholics believe the church can be healed by permitting married priests and the ordination of women. Ardent traditionalists who link homosexuality to sexual abuse see the scandal as a sign that the church must return to a holiness grounded in fealty to traditional teachings. Still others call for a democratization of the church so that bishops, who answer only to Pope John Paul II, will be held accountable by their dioceses.

"We've had so much institutional culture shock that the deeper [question] is where to go from here," said Dennis Doyle, a church historian and professor at the University of Dayton in Ohio, founded by the Marianist teacher order.

A Volatile Debate

The current scandal has struck with unprecedented breadth and fury. . . . Scores of priests from coast to coast and three bishops around the world have resigned, been fired or asked to retire.

So volatile is the debate that rational discussion is impaired. "We are in a dangerous period. . . . Everyone inside and outside the church, wants to find simplistic solutions," wrote Father Stephen J. Rossetti, president of the St. Luke Institute, which treats sexually abusing priests, in . . . the Jesuit magazine *America*.

The church's dilemma lies at the intersection of celibacy, homosexuality and secrecy.

Celibacy

What one often hears is that if an offending priest had a healthy sexual outlet—in other words, a wife—he wouldn't turn to minors for sexual gratification.

But to suggest a direct correlation between celibacy and

the sexual abuse of minors is both facile and specious. Study after study demonstrate that pedophilia, an attraction to pre-pubescent children, and ephebophilia, an attraction to post-pubescent youths, more often involves heterosexual men who are friends or relatives of their victims.

In such cases, the abusers suffer from what psychologists call arrested psychosexual development. They are sexually immature. Often they have difficulty relating to and negotiating with adults. In other cases, they may have experienced feelings of abandonment and low self-esteem.

In other cases, heterosexual men have been known to molest boys, not necessarily because of latent homosexual feelings, but because they were molested when they were young. These are but a few explanations of a complex pathology.

Nonetheless, celibacy can introduce added tensions in the life of a priest who is not psychologically healthy or emotionally mature.

In years past, many priests who later became offenders had moved directly from high school seminaries to graduate seminaries without the usual life experiences common to most other young men.

Once in seminary, their sexual maturity was further impeded as the church inculcated its future priests with the value and necessity of celibacy. Celibacy is seen as a way of "donating" oneself completely to God and to those to whom the priest ministers as an "icon of Christ."

Seminarians have been known to surreptitiously explore their sexuality, but several priests said in interviews with the [Los Angeles] Times that they didn't want to risk their future ordination by getting caught. They waited until after they were ordained. (None of these priests are known to have ever been accused of sexual abuse of minors.)

A Difficult Challenge

Celibacy is difficult under the best of circumstances. Richard Sipe, a former priest who has closely studied the issue, reports that at any given time only 50% of priests are celibate. Over a priest's lifetime, only 2% are consistently celibate, Sipe says.

Though his figures are disputed by many in the church,

few argue that celibacy requires at least two essential factors to work: an authentic spirituality, and nonsexual intimacy with good and trusted friends who may or may not be in the priesthood.

One who has underscored this is Father Donald B. Cozzens, the president-rector of Saint Mary Seminary and Graduate School of Theology in Cleveland.

Cagle. © 2002 by Cagle Cartoons, Inc. Reproduced by permission.

"Paradoxically," Cozzens told the *Times*, "the safest path to an authentic life of celibacy is not to eschew friendship because it's a threat, but to enter into honest relationships that are intimate without being sexual."

Yet for a priest who is not emotionally mature or psychologically healthy, relating to adults and sharing intimate details of his life may be a daunting challenge. He may inappropriately turn to youths to fill his needs for love and intimacy.

In years past, most seminaries did not address issues of human sexuality. That is changing. Most of the priests caught up in the latest scandal are older men, many of them retired. That may be a hopeful sign that more comprehensive psychological screening of seminary applicants and a fuller discussion of sexual issues may be paying off.

But there is no foolproof psychological test to ferret out pedophiles or ephebophiles.

Homosexuality

Many of the recent cases of priestly abuse that have stunned the nation involve post-pubescent boys. Some church critics argued that if homosexual priests were purged, the problem would decline.

This suggestion feeds on an old and disproved stereotype that gay men are more likely to molest youths than heterosexual men. Here, again, experts and leading bishops say retarded psychosexual development, not sexual orientation, is the problem.

Few deny the enormous contributions that priests who are gay continue to make to the life and ministry of the church. It is often said that were they suddenly to leave the scene, the church would be thrown into a crisis. Its current priesthood shortage would be compounded many times over.

Nevertheless, the presence of what is widely viewed as disproportionate numbers of homosexuals in the priesthood has, in some critics' minds, changed the culture of the church. If present ordination trends continue, Sipe predicts, a majority of priests will be homosexuals by 2010.

Theology school president Cozzens said that, based on 36 years in the priesthood, estimates that at least 20% of priests have homosexual orientations are probably understated, although he could not say what the higher figure should be.

Whatever the percentage, bishops in the past have quashed suggestions that the church undertake polls to find out just how many of its priests are homosexual. It is an issue they simply do not want to deal with.

The church does ordain homosexuals. It was long thought that a man's sexual orientation was irrelevant since all priests, straight or gay, are required to live a celibate life.

But gay priests face dilemmas unknown to heterosexual clergy. The church teaches that a homosexual orientation is "objectively disordered" and that homosexual acts are "intrinsically evil." More recently, the pope's Vatican press secretary, Joaquin Navarro-Valls, said the church should not ordain homosexuals and even suggested that the ordination of

119

current homosexual priests may be invalid.

Gay priests learned long ago to remain in the closet. Most feel they could not possibly "come out" to their parishioners and expect to keep their jobs. The tension created by their decision is only part of a culture of secrecy that has bedeviled the church.

The Role of Secrecy

Secrecy, not sexual orientation, is responsible for the depth of the current crisis. Catholics outraged by the sexual abuse at least understood how a priest could fall. But they could not countenance the secrecy of some of their bishops, who knowingly shuffled sexual-abuser priests from parish to parish and left parishioners in the dark.

Though the bishops no doubt believed they were protecting the church from scandal, in retrospect most now realize they did greater damage by not firing wayward priests and being more open with their parishioners. Their most frequent defense has been that psychologists advised them that priests who molested adolescents could be successfully treated.

Resentment of secrecy in the church has given more spirit to long-running contentions among reformers who have called for a bigger voice for the laity in the American church and demanded more accountability from bishops. Other denominations allow churches to hire and fire their clergymen and elect their bishops, but the Catholic hierarchy has zealously guarded those prerogatives.

The secrecy argument leads not only to discussion of accountability but also to the question of whom the church allows to be priests. Liberals argued that women and married men would not have stood for the secrecy of sexual abuse. Nor, they say, would the church's progress in addressing the problem have been so uneven.

"If there were women priests and women bishops and married bishops, the likelihood of this happening in the first place would be close to nil," said Terrance Sweeney of Encino, who left the priesthood to be married. "Men and women who were in positions of authority in the church, who had young children, simply would not have tolerated this. They would not have tolerated the secrecy."

Bishops dispute that. In the last decade, most have put sexual-abuse prevention policies into place, and they have toughened them over the years.

Yet leaders of abuse-victims groups believe it took outside pressures—among them tougher criminal laws requiring the reporting of sexual abuse and costly settlements with victims—to force the church to act.

Periodical Bibliography

The following articles have been selected to supplement the diverse views presented in this chapter.

Sidney Callahan	"Stunted Teaching on Sex Has Role in Church's Crisis," *National Catholic Reporter*, March 21, 2003.
Margaret Carlson	"What the Nuns Didn't Know: Could They Have Uncovered Abuse? Not in a Culture That Kept Them in the Dark," *Time*, April 15, 2002.
Edd Doerr	"A Culture of Clergy Sexual Abuse," *Humanist*, November/December 2003.
Mary Eberstadt	"The Elephant in the Sacristy," *Weekly Standard*, June 17, 2002.
Matthew Felling	"Sex, Lies, and Vaticangate," *World & I*, December 2002.
Kenneth Jost	"Sexual Abuse and the Clergy," *CQ Researcher*, May 3, 2002.
Ann LeBlanc	"Past Imperfect: A Woman Finds Healing and a New Path to God with the Help of an Unlikely Guide," *U.S. Catholic*, October 2003.
Sheryl McCarthy	"The Church Stumbles to Lay Blame on Gays," *Newsday*, April 26, 2002.
Joseph Nicolosi	"A Catholic Psychologist Speaks Out on Homosexuality and the Church," *Wanderer*, June 27, 2002.
John W. O'Malley	"The Scandal: A Historian's Perspective," *America*, May 27, 2002.
Michael Parise	"Betraying the Tender Ideal of the Church: Priests Suffer Because of the Sex Abuse Scandal," *National Catholic Reporter*, May 21, 2004.
John G. Rodwan Jr.	"Priests, the Church, and Special Treatment," *Free Inquiry*, Spring 2003.
Larry B. Stammer	"Most Priests Say Bishops Mishandled Abuse Issue," *Los Angeles Times*, October 20, 2002.
Joann Wypijewski	"The Passion of Father Paul Shanley," *Legal Affairs*, September/October 2004.

CHAPTER 3

Should the Catholic Church Try to Influence Politics and Culture?

Chapter Preface

The role of religion in America's cultural and political discourse has been a subject of increasing controversy in recent years. While the U.S. Constitution forbids governmental sanctioning of any particular religion, influential politicians have often been religious and have incorporated elements of religion in their speeches and in their policy decisions.

Presidential elections, in particular, highlight the debate over the influence of religion on politics. In 1928, for example, Democrat Al Smith became the first Catholic presidential nominee in U.S. history. At the time, many Americans were concerned that a Catholic president's policy decisions would be unduly influenced by the Vatican, and Smith lost the election. About three decades later, in 1960, John F. Kennedy became the second Catholic to accept the Democratic presidential nomination. To allay the apprehension that had plagued Al Smith's campaign, Kennedy promised Americans that his faith would have no bearing on his political decisions: "I believe in an America where the separation of church and state is absolute—where no Catholic prelate would tell the president how to act, and no Protestant minister would tell his parishioners for whom to vote." However, Kennedy also argued that presidential candidates should not have to abandon their religious roots. He stated that "if this election is decided on the basis that 40 million Americans lost their chance of being president on the day they were baptized, then it is the whole nation that will be the loser." Kennedy became the first Catholic to be elected U.S. president.

After the 1973 legalization of abortion in the United States, the question of religion and politics became more complex for Catholic politicians. Opposition to abortion is an important cause for the Catholic Church, and the Catholic hierarchy has repeatedly called on Catholic policy makers to vote against any legislation that increases access to abortions. Many Catholic politicians, however, are pro-choice. They echo Kennedy's arguments when they contend that a politician should not impose his or her personal religious beliefs on a politically diverse constituency. Such was the case in 2004 with Democratic presidential nominee John Kerry, a

Catholic who maintained that he was personally opposed to abortion yet also supported a woman's right to have one. Kerry became the focal point of a renewed debate concerning Vatican influence on American politics. In contrast to the cases of Al Smith and John Kennedy, though, many accused Kerry of deviating too much from the Catholic faith. In addition, a few U.S. bishops announced that they would withhold communion, the central Catholic sacrament, from Kerry and other pro-choice politicians.

Most American bishops disagreed with this decision to deny communion to pro-choice politicians and did not follow suit. Still, the controversy continues to elicit a variety of responses from Catholic commentators. For example, pro-life advocate Joe Gigante supports the denial of communion, arguing that "there is a primacy in the fight to end abortion. . . . All other rights are irrelevant if you don't have the right to live. What do . . . other issues like poverty or health care mean to the 44 million children who have died [due to abortion]? But political columnist Andrew Sullivan disagrees, noting that "it is one thing for the church to preach what it believes—the sanctity of unborn human life. It is another thing to use the sacraments of the church to enforce political uniformity on the matter."

In the following chapter, contributors examine further the influence of the Catholic Church in today's political and cultural controversies.

"Catholic public officials who consistently support abortion on demand are cooperating with evil in a public manner."

The Church Should Deny Communion to Catholic Politicians Who Oppose Church Teachings

John Donoghue, Robert Baker, and Peter Jugis

In the following viewpoint Catholic bishops John Donoghue, Robert Baker, and Peter Jugis announce their intention to deny communion to Catholic politicians who disagree with church teachings, such as those who support pro-abortion legislation. A fundamental teaching of the church is respect for the sacredness of human life from conception onwards; therefore, the church maintains that laws allowing abortion are intrinsically unjust and immoral. Catholic public officials who support abortion rights are in a state of grave sin—a condition that disqualifies them from receiving communion, the bishops contend. Donoghue is the archbishop of Atlanta, Georgia; Baker is the bishop of Charleston, South Carolina; and Jugis is the bishop of Charlotte, North Carolina.

As you read, consider the following questions:
1. According to the bishops, what dispositions are required for a Catholic to receive communion?
2. What would an abortion-supporting Catholic politician need to do in order to receive communion again, according to the authors?

John Donoghue, Robert Baker, and Peter Jugis, "A Manifest Lack of Proper Disposition for Holy Communion," *Origins*, vol. 34, September 2, 2004, pp. 188–89. Copyright © 2004 by John Donoghue, Robert Baker, and Peter Jugis. Reproduced by permission.

As bishops, we have the obligation to teach and guide the Catholic faithful whom we shepherd in the body of Christ. A fundamental teaching of our church is respect for the sacred gift of life. This teaching flows from the natural law and from divine revelation.

Life is a gift bestowed upon us by God, a truth underscored by the commandment: "You shall not kill" (Dt. 5:17). The Old Testament also teaches us that human life in the womb is precious to God: "I formed you in the womb" (Jer. 1:5). The right to life is a value "which no individual, no majority and no state can ever create, modify or destroy but must only acknowledge, respect and promote" (Pope John Paul II, *Evangelium Vitae*, 71a). A law, therefore, which legitimizes the direct killing of innocent human beings through abortion is intrinsically unjust, since it is directly opposed to the natural law, to God's revealed commandments and to the consequent right of every individual to possess life from the moment of conception to the moment of natural death.

The Responsibility of Catholic Politicians

Catholics in political life have the responsibility to exemplify in their public service this teaching of the church and to work for the protection of all innocent life. There can be no contradiction between the values bestowed by baptism and the Catholic faith, and the public expression of those values. Catholic public officials who consistently support abortion on demand are cooperating with evil in a public manner. By supporting pro-abortion legislation they participate in manifest grave sin, a condition which excludes them from admission to holy communion as long as they persist in the pro-abortion stance (cf. Canon 915).

Holy communion is where Catholics meet as a family in Christ, united by a common faith. Every Catholic is responsible for being properly prepared for this profound union with Christ. Participation in holy communion requires certain dispositions on the part of the communicant, namely, perseverance in the life of grace and communion in the faith of the church, in the sacraments and in the hierarchical order of the church (Pope John Paul II, *Ecclesia de Eucharistia*, 35–38).

The church also recognizes that there is a manifest lack of a proper disposition for holy communion in those whose outward conduct is "seriously, clearly and steadfastly contrary" to the church's moral teaching (*Ecclesia de Eucharistia*, 37b). A manifest lack of proper disposition for holy communion is found to be present in those who consistently support pro-abortion legislation. Because support for pro-abortion legislation is gravely sinful, such persons should not be admitted to holy communion.

The Proper Disposition for Communion

We also take this opportunity to address all Catholics whose beliefs and conduct do not correspond to the Gospel and to church teaching. To receive the great gift of God—the body, blood, soul and divinity of our Lord Jesus Christ—we must approach holy communion free from mortal sin. Those who are conscious of being in a state of grave sin should avail themselves of the sacrament of reconciliation [confession] before coming to holy communion. To partake of the eucharist is to partake of Christ himself, and to enter into sacramental communion with our Lord we must all be properly disposed.

Because of the influence that Catholics in public life have on the conduct of our daily lives and on the formation of our nation's future, we declare that Catholics serving in public life espousing positions contrary to the teaching of the church on the sanctity and inviolability of human life, especially those running for or elected to public office, are not to be admitted to holy communion in any Catholic church within our jurisdictions: the Archdiocese of Atlanta, the dioceses of Charleston and Charlotte. Only after reconciliation with the church has occurred, with the knowledge and consent of the local bishop, and public disavowal of former support for procured abortion, will the individual be permitted to approach the sacrament of the holy eucharist.

We undertake this action to safeguard the sacred dignity of the most holy sacrament of the altar, to reassure the faithful and to save sinners.

"[Catholic politicians who disagree with Church teachings] can either relinquish the political arena . . . or they can defy the church. Surely each position is untenable."

The Church Should Not Deny Communion to Catholic Politicians Who Oppose Church Teachings

Joan Chittister

In the viewpoint that follows, Joan Chittister questions the recent decision of several American bishops to deny communion to Catholic politicians who do not vote in accordance with approved Catholic teachings. If this were to become a trend, she argues, Catholic politicians would be forced to make one of the following choices: ignore alternative opinions on complex political issues or leave the church. Either option would cause Americans to become wary of electing Catholic politicians, which would weaken the church's voice in public discussions about moral issues, Chittister maintains. While the church should offer guidance, it should not dictate how people should vote, she concludes. Author, lecturer, and activist Chittister is a Benedictine sister residing in Erie, Pennsylvania.

As you read, consider the following questions:

1. According to Chittister, what is "the Catholic question"?
2. About how many Catholics serve in the U.S. Congress and state legislatures, according to Chittister?

Joan Chittister, "Church, Conscience, Constitution, and Common Sense: We Thought It Was Resolved in 1960, but in 2004 the 'Catholic Question' Is Back with a Vengeance," *National Catholic Reporter*, vol. 40, May 7, 2004, pp. 17–18. Copyright © 2004 by the *National Catholic Reporter*. Reproduced by permission of the author.

John Kerry went to Mass and Communion last week [in May 2004].[1] At one time, that would have been considered admirable by Catholics and non-Catholics alike. Now it stands on the brink of being a serious political question and, perhaps, an even more serious Catholic question.

Call it what you will—dilemma, muddle, mess or quandary —but the results are all the same: We are facing a situation in the American Catholic church and American politics that may be more serious than anything we have dealt with in years.

The Catholic Question

You remember the Catholic question. This is the subject that defeated Catholic presidential candidate Al Smith in 1936. It's the concern that plagued John F. Kennedy's presidential candidacy in 1960. It's the issue we thought the election of 1960 resolved, in fact. And . . . in 2004, [it came back] with a vengeance.

This Catholic question is not about vouchers for Catholic schools, as in, "Can a state grant them in a country built on the separation of church and state?"[2] In that case, the bishops of the church stayed ominously silent about the morality of the Vietnam War and chose instead to melt into the mainstream in the hope, many argued, of receiving financial aid for the then-ailing Catholic school system. No public moral questions were asked.

It's also not about the validity of conscientious objection in the Catholic tradition, as in, "Is it authentic for a Catholic to refuse military service on the grounds that being Catholic justifies a citizen's refusal to fight and kill for the sake of the state?" In that case, the just war tradition and the bishops' peace pastoral of 1983 gave new credence to that position and called on Catholics to make conscientious decisions about their participation in war, though the document itself did not outlaw war, not even nuclear war.

It's not about whether Catholic politicians can own slaves or vote to maintain segregation, an issue about which the

1. Kerry, a Democratic senator from Massachusetts, was the Democratic presidential nominee in 2004.   2. Vouchers are state-funded grants that help pay tuition at private or religious schools.

church once theologized so adroitly.

It's not about the death penalty and the continuing commitment of the United States to deter murder by murdering people, which is surely also a pro-life question.

And it's not, at least not completely, about "Rum, Romanism and Rebellion," the political slogan that purported to describe the Democratic Party in 1884—the year of the "dirtiest election in U.S. politics"—as too Catholic, too beholden to Vatican directions, to be entrusted with the presidency of a pluralistic nation.

The Election of 2004

But the election of 2004, if we're not careful, could easily . . . revolve around the "Catholic question" again, about whether or not the Catholic church directs the way Catholic candidates vote on public issues.

This election is not about whether the church should lead the discussion of the moral evaluation of any of these things. On the contrary. Never have we needed moral guidance more than we do in a society where science has now changed life and changed death, changed family and changed sex, changed birth and changed creation.

But this election is about whether or not a Catholic can be a politician, exercise a Catholic conscience in a pluralistic world, and stay a practicing Catholic at the same time. The implications of those questions for Catholics, for Catholic political figures, for the Catholic church and, eventually, for the country itself are immeasurable. This one could decide the role of Catholics in both church and state for years to come.

A Troubling Dilemma

John Kennedy's famous answer to the Southern Baptist Convention's concern about the relationship between a Catholic candidate and the Vatican seemed to answer the question once and for all. "I believe in an America," he said, "where no public official either requests or accepts instructions on public policy from the pope, the National Council of Churches or any other ecclesiastical source—where no religious body seeks to impose its will directly or indirectly upon the general populace or the public acts of its officials."

Now, with the position of a few bishops that Catholic politicians who do not vote in accordance with Catholic teaching cannot receive the Eucharist, the dilemma is obvious: Catholic politicians have one of two choices. They can either relinquish the political arena to the rest of the body politic or they can defy the church. Surely each position is untenable, illogical and destructive of both the church and the place of the Catholic vision of life in the public arena.

Pro-Choice Politicians and Communion

Would you support or oppose the Catholic Church denying communion to Catholic politicians who are in favor of legal abortion?

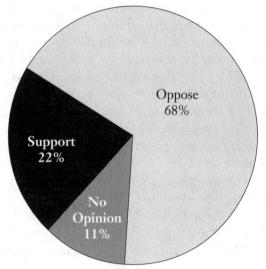

Oppose
68%

Support
22%

No
Opinion
11%

ABC News/*Washington Post* poll, May 2004.

Put in this kind of situation, Catholic politicians—[more than 140] Catholics now serve in Congress and [more than 400] in state legislatures—will have to go to their respective houses and senates with their minds already made up on current topics. They will have to refuse to consider alternate arguments about how to approach complex issues—even though many churches are engaged in moral analysis of these same issues, as once they were on the very issue of separation of church and state.

Echoes of the Middle Ages may well be heard in the land. Catholics who run for office will be immediately suspect again and perhaps as unelectable as they were in the past.

And, even more serious than that, the discussions of moral alternatives at the highest levels of power will include everything but the Catholic tradition. Will factor it out. On purpose. Consciously. In general. And by our own hands. Surely we have enough indication right now of what could be the long-term moral effects of that on a multitude of subjects to cancel any move in that direction.

Diminishing the Church's Influence

The second option for Catholic politicians in a climate such as this, if the trend to excommunication continues, is that they can simply leave the church. Then the notion that Catholicism—the church—is incompatible with human development, discovery and thought will be modeled at the highest levels for the whole world to see. Then the real influence of the church itself on the human spirit, perhaps on Catholics in general, can only be diminished. Then we will lose a great deal more than a few individual politicians.

From where I stand, it seems to me that giving good moral guidance and allowing the voting population to make its own decisions at the polls about whether or not a given position is moral and a given candidate a worthy legislator will have more effect in the long run on the development of the country—and the church—than selective coercion can possibly have now. The issue right now is not the issues themselves. It is how far a tactic like this will go.

To be honest, I have often wanted bishops to take a stronger stand on certain issues: the women's issue and its effect on half the human race, or the nuclear issue and its effect on the life of the planet, or the [2003] war in Iraq and its effect on the life and safety of civilians—some of whom might even possibly be pregnant. But I don't think excommunication is the way to do it. Not if conscience, constitution and even the integrity and development of the church really mean anything at all.

"The Church teaches that respect for homosexual persons cannot lead in any way to approval of homosexual behaviour or to legal recognition of homosexual unions."

The Catholic Church Should Oppose Homosexual Marriage

Congregation for the Doctrine of the Faith

The Congregation for the Doctrine of the Faith is an office of the Roman curia (the governing bureaucracy of the Catholic Church) that is responsible for safeguarding Catholic faith and morals. In the following viewpoint the congregation maintains that the church must oppose homosexual marriage because homosexual activity is unnatural and intrinsically immoral. Marriage was instituted by God as a union between sexually complementary persons—male and female—who are able to procreate, the authors argue. They contend that legalizing homosexual unions would radically undermine the traditional concept of marriage and family and cause great damage to society. The congregation concludes, furthermore, that it is the duty of Catholic politicians to openly oppose homosexual marriage.

As you read, consider the following questions:

1. According to the authors, what virtue are homosexuals called to live?
2. Why does the church oppose the adoption of children by homosexual couples, according to the authors?
3. What specific advice does the Congregation for the Doctrine of the Faith have for Catholic lawmakers?

Congregation for the Doctrine of the Faith, "Considerations Regarding Proposals to Give Legal Recognition to Unions Between Homosexual Persons," www.vatican.va, June 3, 2003.

Homosexuality is a troubling moral and social phenomenon, even in those countries where it does not present significant legal issues. It gives rise to greater concern in those countries that have granted or intend to grant—legal recognition to homosexual unions, which may include the possibility of adopting children. The present Considerations [are] . . . aimed at protecting and promoting the dignity of marriage, the foundation of the family, and the stability of society, of which this institution is a constitutive element. The present Considerations are also intended to give direction to Catholic politicians by indicating the approaches to proposed legislation in this area which would be consistent with Christian conscience. Since this question relates to the natural moral law, the arguments that follow are addressed not only to those who believe in Christ, but to all persons committed to promoting and defending the common good of society.

The Nature of Marriage

The Church's teaching on marriage and on the complementarity of the sexes reiterates a truth that is evident to right reason and recognized as such by all the major cultures of the world. Marriage is not just any relationship between human beings. It was established by the Creator with its own nature, essential properties and purpose. No ideology can erase from the human spirit the certainty that marriage exists solely between a man and a woman, who by mutual personal gift, proper and exclusive to themselves, tend toward the communion of their persons. In this way, they mutually perfect each other, in order to cooperate with God in the procreation and upbringing of new human lives.

The natural truth about marriage was confirmed by the Revelation contained in the biblical accounts of creation, an expression also of the original human wisdom, in which the voice of nature itself is heard. There are three fundamental elements of the Creator's plan for marriage, as narrated in the Book of Genesis.

In the first place, man, the image of God, was created "male and female" (*Gen* 1:27). Men and women are equal as persons and complementary as male and female. Sexuality is something that pertains to the physical-biological realm and has also been raised to a new level—the personal level—where nature and spirit are united.

Marriage is instituted by the Creator as a form of life in which a communion of persons is realized involving the use of the sexual faculty. "That is why a man leaves his father and mother and clings to his wife and they become one flesh" (*Gen* 2:24).

Third, God has willed to give the union of man and woman a special participation in his work of creation. Thus, he blessed the man and the woman with the words "Be fruitful and multiply" (*Gen* 1:28). Therefore, in the Creator's plan, sexual complementarity and fruitfulness belong to the very nature of marriage.

Furthermore, the marital union of man and woman has been elevated by Christ to the dignity of a sacrament. . . .

Against the Natural Moral Law

There are absolutely no grounds for considering homosexual unions to be in any way similar or even remotely analogous to God's plan for marriage and family. Marriage is holy, while homosexual acts go against the natural moral law. [According to the Catechism of the Catholic Church] homosexual acts "close the sexual act to the gift of life. They do not proceed from a genuine affective and sexual complementarity. Under no circumstances can they be approved".

Sacred Scripture condemns homosexual acts "a serious depravity . . . This judgment of Scripture does not of course permit us to conclude that all those who suffer from this anomaly are personally responsible for it, but it does attest to the fact that homosexual acts are intrinsically disordered". This same moral judgment is found in many Christian writers of the first centuries and is unanimously accepted by Catholic Tradition.

Nonetheless, according to the teaching of the Church, men and women with homosexual tendencies "must be accepted with respect, compassion and sensitivity. Every sign of unjust discrimination in their regard should be avoided". They are called, like other Christians, to live the virtue of chastity. The homosexual inclination is however "objectively disordered" and homosexual practices are "sins gravely contrary to chastity".

Faced with the fact of homosexual unions, civil authorities adopt different positions. At times they simply tolerate the phenomenon; at other times they advocate legal recognition of such unions, under the pretext of avoiding, with regard to certain rights, discrimination against persons who live with someone of the same sex. In other cases, they favour giving homosexual unions legal equivalence to marriage properly so-called, along with the legal possibility of adopting children. . . .

Homosexual Acts Cannot Be Approved

Homosexuality refers to relations between men or between women who experience an exclusive or predominant sexual attraction toward persons of the same sex. It has taken a great variety of forms through the centuries and in different cultures. Its psychological genesis remains largely unexplained. Basing itself on Sacred Scripture, which presents homosexual acts as acts of grave depravity, tradition has always declared that "homosexual acts are intrinsically disordered." They are contrary to the natural law. They close the sexual act to the gift of life. They do not proceed from a genuine affective and sexual complementarity. Under no circumstances can they be approved.

Catechism of the Catholic Church, English Translation, 1994.

In those situations where homosexual unions have been legally recognized or have been given the legal status and rights belonging to marriage, clear and emphatic opposition is a duty. One must refrain from any kind of formal cooperation in the enactment or application of such gravely unjust laws and, as far as possible, from material cooperation on the level of their application. In this area, everyone can exercise the right to conscientious objection. . . .

Arguments Against Legal Recognition

Homosexual unions are totally lacking in the biological and anthropological elements of marriage and family which would be the basis, on the level of reason, for granting them legal recognition. Such unions are not able to contribute in a proper way to the procreation and survival of the human race.

The possibility of using recently discovered methods of artificial reproduction, beyond involving a grave lack of respect for human dignity, does nothing to alter this inadequacy.

Homosexual unions are also totally lacking in the conjugal dimension, which represents the human and ordered form of sexuality. Sexual relations are human when and insofar as they express and promote the mutual assistance of the sexes in marriage and are open to the transmission of new life.

As experience has shown, the absence of sexual complementarity in these unions creates obstacles in the normal development of children who would be placed in the care of such persons. They would be deprived of the experience of either fatherhood or motherhood. Allowing children to be adopted by persons living in such unions would actually mean doing violence to these children, in the sense that their condition of dependency would be used to place them in an environment that is not conducive to their full human development. This is gravely immoral and in open contradiction to the principle, recognized also in the United Nations Convention on the Rights of the Child, that the best interests of the child, as the weaker and more vulnerable party, are to be the paramount consideration in every case.

A Grave Detriment

Society owes its continued survival to the family, founded on marriage. The inevitable consequence of legal recognition of homosexual unions would be the redefinition of marriage, which would become, in its legal status, an institution devoid of essential reference to factors linked to heterosexuality; for example, procreation and raising children. If, from the legal standpoint, marriage between a man and a woman were to be considered just one possible form of marriage, the concept of marriage would undergo a radical transformation, with grave detriment to the common good. By putting homosexual unions on a legal plane analogous to that of marriage and the family, the State acts arbitrarily and in contradiction with its duties.

The principles of respect and non-discrimination cannot be invoked to support legal recognition of homosexual unions. Differentiating between persons or refusing social recognition or benefits is unacceptable only when it is contrary to justice. The denial of the social and legal status of marriage to forms of cohabitation that are not and cannot be marital is not opposed to justice; on the contrary, justice requires it. . . .

Not even in a remote analogous sense do homosexual unions fulfil the purpose for which marriage and family deserve specific categorical recognition. On the contrary, there are good reasons for holding that such unions are harmful to the proper development of human society, especially if their impact on society were to increase. . . .

Catholic Politicians

If it is true that all Catholics are obliged to oppose the legal recognition of homosexual unions, Catholic politicians are obliged to do so in a particular way, in keeping with their responsibility as politicians. Faced with legislative proposals in favour of homosexual unions, Catholic politicians are to take account of the following ethical indications.

When legislation in favour of the recognition of homosexual unions is proposed for the first time in a legislative assembly, the Catholic law-maker has a moral duty to express his opposition clearly and publicly and to vote against it. To vote in favour of a law so harmful to the common good is gravely immoral.

When legislation in favour of the recognition of homosexual unions is already in force, the Catholic politician must oppose it in the ways that are possible for him and make his opposition known; it is his duty to witness to the truth. . . .

The Church teaches that respect for homosexual persons cannot lead in any way to approval of homosexual behaviour or to legal recognition of homosexual unions. The common good requires that laws recognize, promote and protect marriage as the basis of the family, the primary unit of society. Legal recognition of homosexual unions or placing them on the same level as marriage would mean not only the approval of deviant behaviour, with the consequence of making it a model in present-day society, but would also obscure basic values which belong to the common inheritance of humanity. The Church cannot fail to defend these values, for the good of men and women and for the good of society itself.

*"Just as the Vatican came reluctantly . . .
to the truth that the earth does indeed
revolve round the sun, so too it ought to
listen to science about homosexuality."*

The Church Should Not Oppose Homosexual Marriage

Matthew Fox

The Catholic Church's opposition to gay marriage is based on outdated theology, argues Matthew Fox in the following viewpoint. Because church authorities have not seriously considered recent scientific evidence proving that homosexuality is natural, they continue to condemn gay unions as deviant and evil, Fox points out. He maintains that since it is natural for homosexuals to love others of the same gender, the church should be supportive by encouraging monogamy and stable relationships for gays and lesbians. Celebrating gay and lesbian unions would be a way of honoring the diversity of creation, he concludes. Fox, president of Wisdom University in Oakland, California, is the author of dozens of books, including *Original Blessing* and *The Coming of the Cosmic Christ*.

As you read, consider the following questions:

1. In what way does the church's stance on homosexuality constitute "a new Galileo case," according to Fox?
2. According to the author, how many other animal species have homosexual populations?
3. How might homosexual love serve as a way to help save the human species, in Fox's opinion?

Matthew Fox, "The Vatican's Condemnation of Gay Marriage: Another Galileo Case in the Making," *Catholic New Times*, vol. 27, September 7, 2003, pp. 10–11. Copyright © 2003 by Catholic New Times, Inc. Reproduced by permission.

Editor's Note: This viewpoint was written before the death of Pope John Paul II in April 2005. Later that month, Cardinal Joseph Ratzinger was elected as Pope Benedict XVI.

The present papacy [of John Paul II] has prided itself on removing the condemnation of Galileo Galilei, which hung in the air for 359 years. In 1992, at the time of the lifting of his condemnation for heresy and the admission that the earth does indeed revolve around the sun, [John Paul II] told the Academy of Sciences that "the underlying problems of this case concern both the nature of science and the message of faith. One day we may find ourselves in a similar situation, which will require both sides to have an informed awareness of the field and of the limits of their own competencies."

This "one day" may have arrived. I speak of the pope's and Cardinal Ratzinger's recent condemnation of homosexual unions. In the twelve-page document called *Considerations Regarding Proposals To Give Legal Recognition to Unions Between Homosexual Persons*, there is not one reference to any scientific discussion of homosexuality, not a single note of awareness of the fact that thirty years ago the American Psychiatric Association, for example, deleted the issue of homosexuality from its Diagnostic and Statistical Manual of Mental Disorders. In fact, the papal document calls homosexuality "deviant behaviour" and "evil."

What is most telling about this document is that its entire argument is built on an appeal to "natural moral law" so much so that the document claims to speak not just to Roman Catholics but to all people "committed to promoting and defending the common good of society." And yet the only arguments given for "natural moral law" are from Scripture. Not a word from science. There are four footnotes to a catechism—not one to any serious study about homosexuality.

Medieval Science?

This is why, using the very pope's argument concerning Galileo, we have here a new Galileo case, one that demonstrates the church lacking an "informed awareness of the field and of the limits of its own competencies." Will we have to wait another 400 years to hear a pope apologize anew? The only "science" implicit in this condemnation of homosexuality is medieval science.

As for the use of Scripture, it should be noted that the historical Jesus said not one recorded word about homosexuality. The three references to Saint Paul in this document should be taken with a heavy dose of salt. Why? Because Paul is the same author who declared that "slaves should obey their masters." This kind of theology was invoked *ad nauseam* in the nineteenth century to support slavery. One of the scholarly achievements of our time has been to distinguish the words of the historical Jesus from those of the theologian Paul who is sometimes right on and some times way off the mark. It is scandalous that the Vatican has ignored its Biblical homework as much as its scientific homework.

Just as the Vatican came reluctantly and ever so slowly to the truth that the earth does indeed revolve round the sun, so too it ought to listen to science about homosexuality. The facts are these: About 10 per cent of any given human population is going to be homosexual. Furthermore, we now know that at least 64 other species have homosexual populations including dolphins, cranes, many birds and others. So the medieval argument that homosexuality is "unnatural" or "contrary to natural law" and which is the entire basis for this papal document—is simply medieval science. It is not today's science. Popes and Inquisitors would do well to know the "limits of their own competencies" as the pope put it while resuscitating Galileo.

Gays and Natural Law

The fact is that being gay and expressing one's love for another of the same sex is natural for gay and lesbian people. They are following the "natural law" by so doing. (Heterosexual marriage would be "unnatural" for them and does not work.) Nature has made them gay. A church that wants to teach love ought to be encouraging monogamous and established relationships of love instead of forcing gay people into self-hatred and sometimes into practices of promiscuity that separate love from sexual expression.

As for the "common good," it should be noted that the common good is served in various ways by gay and lesbian people and their extraordinary gift in the arts is just one such gift. Does the pope pray in the Sistine Chapel? Does Cardinal Ratzinger visit there? A gay man did it! Michelangelo and many artistic geniuses through the ages have been gay.

Furthermore, this document claims that the purpose of marriage is to have children and that having children is the way the human race is to save itself. Here too the Vatican might do well to read today's science. There are too many humans on the planet, not too few. Ways of birth control, including homosexual love, are ways to save our species and other species as well.

The Need for a Deeper Listening

With another scandal having erupted, . . . in the area of sex, Catholics are again demanding a greater involvement in their Church. That it is being resisted not only by an [aging] pope [John Paul II] but also by the like-minded bishops he has appointed, should surprise no one. Patriarchy dies hard. And accepting new insights and understandings on the natural law may be just as hard. At a minimum . . . we can say that the lack of updated Vatican thinking on biology, natural law and the diversity in creation is problematic. And the language around homosexual persons [as] "deviant and evil" we find unfortunate and offensive. . . .

Catholic theology increasingly must be seen to be open to ongoing creation, redemption and sanctification. The times call for deeper listening, in particular to the experience of homosexual people.

Catholic New Times, September 7, 2003.

It is interesting that the papal document, which also condemns the adoption of children by gays, appeared at the moment of the Supreme Court decision removing homosexual acts as felonies. And at the time that the Episcopal Church wrestled publicly and courageously with the issue of ordaining an out-of-the-closet gay man as bishop. God bless the Episcopal Church for its right practice. God pray for the Vatican and others who think the gay issue is a scriptural one when it is in fact an issue of nature and creation and our knowing more about both. It was the inability to comprehend a non-literal reading of Scripture and its "inability to disassociate itself from an age-old cosmology," according to the Papal commission on Galileo, that resulted in his condemnation. Protestant Biblical advocates should take notice.

Diversity and Creation

Thomas Aquinas who is referenced in this document, himself wrote 700 years ago that "a mistake about creation results in a mistake about God." Mistakes about creation happen when we ignore science whose job it is to examine creation. The mistakes about creation that are so plentiful in this document will lead people into mistakes about God. Instead of holding our breath for another 400 years while the Vatican gets its head out of its catechisms and starts learning what science has learned about homosexuality, it would be wise to put one's energy into praising the amazing and beautiful diversity that the Creator has put into her creation, a diversity that includes homosexual love along with all the other kinds of love that course through humanity and other earthlings. Instead of condemning the Divine Imagination we might do well to start imitating it. Instead of condemning kinds of love that may be different from our own, we ought to celebrate it and be busier about putting our own houses and hearts of love in order.

"The present disorientation and dysfunction of our society, and of the individuals who people it, was predicted by many people who anticipated the widespread acceptance of contraception."

The Catholic Church Should Continue to Oppose Artificial Contraception

Catholic Insight

The widespread acceptance of artificial birth control has led to a dysfunctional society, argue the editors of *Catholic Insight* in the following viewpoint. Contraception, which separates the sexual act from its natural reproductive purpose, encourages people to pursue self-centered sexual pleasure, the authors contend. They maintain, furthermore, that this self-absorbed sexual ethic has led to other kinds of immorality, such as the rejection of marriage and family, the acceptance of abortion, and the rise of the homosexual rights movement. *Catholic Insight* is a monthly Canadian journal of conservative Catholic opinion.

As you read, consider the following questions:
1. In the opinion of *Catholic Insight*, how is contraception linked to the "homosexualization of heterosexuality"?
2. What influential leaders and thinkers were opposed to contraception, according to the authors?
3. In what year did the Catholic Church officially oppose artificial contraception, according to *Catholic Insight*?

*C*atholic Insight came across the following reflection in a circular letter sent around by Father Tony Van Hee, S.J., the priest who witnesses to the prolife cause on Parliament Hill in Ottawa [Canada], year after year.

It presents the main points of an essay by Patrick F. Fagan of the Heritage Foundation in Washington called "A Culture of Inverted Sexuality", subtitled, "Contraception has begotten a trend which might be characterized as the 'homosexualization' of heterosexuality". It appeared in the November 1998 issue of the *Catholic World Report*. It chronicles how "[c]ontraception has radically changed the social function of the sexual act" in North America and Western Europe. We have followed Fr. Van Hee's quotes and summaries but added some subtitles.

Mr. Fagan begins his essay as follows:

It is impossible to look at the changes in our culture over the last few decades without realizing the extent of the changes wrought by the new sexual mores. The thesis of this essay is that the strength of the present homosexual movement and the other radical sexual movements is rooted in these changes.

Twentieth Century

Major changes in thought on the nature of the sexual act began in the latter part of the 19th century, gathered steam in the early part of [the twentieth] century, and achieved a significant breakthrough in 1930 with the breakdown of the unified tradition of Christian religious-moral teaching on the nature of the sexual act.

By the late 1940s American married couples were contracepting in growing numbers. By the 1960s the children of these contracepting couples became the leaders of the sexual revolution, rejecting the need for marriage as the context for the sexual act—a rejection logically based on their experiences. By the 1970s the next generation had enshrined a "woman's right to choose" abortion, thus making it legally possible to be rid of the natural fruit of the sexual act. A generation later, in the 1990s, we have seen the rise of the homosexual-rights movement.

Cause

All of these gradual "slouchings towards Gomorrah" are the natural byproduct of the severing of the sexual act from the prime end of that act, and from its fundamental natural function: the beget-

ting of the child. That severance changes the focus of the sexual act and in doing so changes the adults who so act, both in their own psychological dispositions and in their interpersonal relations. From being ultimately "other focused," sexual mores become "self focused;" from extroversion, sexual affairs move toward introversion; from hetero-focused they become auto-focused.

If one severs the possibility of reproduction from the nature of the sexual act, then it will be difficult to deny the "right" to engage in legally sanctioned sexual activities to those (homosexuals and others) whose sexual act always precludes the begetting of a child.

If homosexuals further argue that they are deprived of an equal right to the pursuit of pleasure—which they say they cannot derive from heterosexual acts—their argument takes on still more force.

Consequently many Protestant churches and government bodies have begun to conclude that homosexuals have a "right" to sanctioned unions: to same-sex "marriages". Under the changed sexual mores that now dominate our culture, it is difficult to deny the persuasiveness of their argument. . . .

The Power of the Sexual Act

The thesis of this essay is not new, Mr. Fagan goes on to say. It is anchored not in any religious doctrine but rather in a natural-law understanding of the power of the sexual act. For countless generations, wise men have recognized the ability of sexual attitudes and activities to orient or disorient not only the individual, but the whole of society. The present disorientation and dysfunction of our society, and of the individuals who people it, was predicted by many people who anticipated the widespread acceptance of contraception. The accuracy of their predictions gives their underlying insights a serious claim to validity.

We can find similar messages coming from many different quarters. For example:

Theodore Roosevelt wrote, "Birth control is the one sin for which the penalty is national death, race death; a sin for which there is no atonement." ['Culture of death' is, therefore, truly an appropriate description.]

Sigmund Freud—no friend of religion—and Mahatma Gandhi are also quoted, warning of the dangers of contraception.

The author continues:

Notice, by the way, that all of the social and psychological disorders described above [but not included here for brevity's sake]—the broken homes, the child abuse, and so forth—are present within the "heterosexual culture". While it is true that the "gay" subculture shows even higher levels of dysfunction on comparable issues, the culture of sexual inversion is not confined to homosexuality. Among heterosexuals, too, the transformation of sexual activity into a self-absorbed process—sustained by no commitment to children or to a spouse—has produced disastrous social and psychological results. . . .

Anglican Turn-About

One of the public functions of religion is to shore up society's adherence to the natural moral law. When the institution of religion caves in on a moral issue, the other institutions (family, education, government, and the marketplace) cannot be expected to maintain the societal defenses.

The family-planning movement, the vehicle for the advancement of contraception, had its roots not only outside of Christianity, but among groups that were quite actively hostile to Christianity. The attack on Christian tradition was already well advanced early in [the twentieth] century. By the same time, the birth-control movement recognized the need to achieve some sort of religious sanction—and had even acquired a primary target for its lobbying efforts. In 1919 the Anglican divine C.K. Millard wrote in *The Modern Churchman*:

Although many Malthusians [followers of population controller Thomas R. Malthus, Anglican parson and economist, 1766–1834] are rationalists, they are well aware that without some religious sanction their policy could never emerge from the dim underworld of unmentioned and unrespected things and could never be advocated openly in the light of day. To this end birth control is camouflaged by pseudo-religious phraseology, and the Anglican Church is asked to alter her teaching. Birth controllers realize that it is useless to ask this of the Catholic Church but as regards the Church of England, which makes no claim to infallibility, the case is different, and discussion is possible.

If a single date could be identified as marking the historical break from the Christian consensus on traditional natural-law principles of sexual morality—if one desired to highlight the West's very first official step down the slippery slope—then August 15, 1930, must be chosen as that unhappy date. That was the day when the Lambeth Conference of the Church of England, by a vote of 193 to 67, approved a resolution which read in part: "Where there is a clearly felt moral obligation to limit or avoid parenthood, . . . and where there is a morally sound reason for avoiding complete abstinence, the Conference agrees that other methods may be used. . . ."

Contraception Trivializes Sex

Contraception allows sexual partners to go through the motions of being intimate without being truly intimate, that is, unreservedly and unconditionally so. The fact that contraception is perfectly in accord with the dominant tone of an alienated society means that the general populace scarcely notices its intrusion upon their intimacy, and seems unaware of contraception's connection to the trivialization of sex, the weakening of marriage, the increase in infidelity, and the dependence on abortion.

Donald DeMarco, *New Oxford Review*, September 1998.

With that vote, the traditional moral unity of Christendom on this issue was broken.

Just as the acceptance of contraception in 1930 was a turning point on sexual morality in Western society, so the rejection of Pope Paul VI's Encyclical Letter on Human Life in 1968, opposing contraception, was a turning point within the Catholic Church, all of us deceived by Satan "disguised as an angel of light" (1 Cor 11:14), like our earthly mother Eve eating the forbidden fruit because it "was good to eat and pleasing to the eye, and . . . desirable for the knowledge that it could give" (Gen 3:6,22).

An Inverted Sexuality

The author of the essay concludes:

The current public debate on homosexuality . . . can be expressed in fairly simple terms. If heterosexual people cannot take on the responsibilities implied by heterosexuality, how can they ask the homosexually inclined person to take on the burden of his struggle for chastity? If the heterosexuals distort the relationship between man and woman at its most intimate level, through their decision to avoid begetting new life, how can they reasonably ask those who are oriented differently to resist their own particular temptation to distort their own lives?

In fact, the mainstream of "heterosexual America" today is now perilously close, in its attitudes and its orientations, to matching the symptoms that lie at the very heart of the homosexual affective disorder: the inversion into the self. The United States has created a culture of rejection, which is incapable of providing the antidote to the homosexual culture. Heterosexuals cannot affirm the sexual humanity of husband and wife while (at the same time) denying its fruit. The child-fearing, child-rejecting heterosexual community cannot but affirm the homosexual in his more complex cry for acceptance and love. Heterosexuals who insist on arrested sexual development for themselves cannot help but condone the same behaviour when it is exhibited among homosexuals.

The massive social and psychological disorder we see all around us is not the making of the "gay community". Our current problems—including even the "gay rights" movement itself—arose as a result of disorders that first became prevalent among heterosexuals. If we want to take the mote out of our "gay" brothers' eyes maybe we should first remove the beam from our own. If we are to develop the attitude of love and affection that is central to helping members of the "gay culture" overcome their inversion, then we Americans must first recover our understanding of the relationship between love, sexuality, and permanent commitment to spouse and children. We must first acknowledge the children each of us has been called to "co-create" and to love, and we must show our love both for those children who are already in this world and for those who may yet come to be. Otherwise, if the two inversions—heterosexual and homosexual—continue to compound each other, the future is bleak indeed—especially for children, and for the society those children will be capable of building.

> *"To maintain, falsely, that [condoms] are ineffective in order to discourage their use is truly immoral. If not insane."*

The Catholic Church's Opposition to Condom Use Is Immoral

Katha Pollitt

Catholic officials have joined fundamentalist Protestants in spreading misinformation about condoms, argues Katha Pollitt in the following viewpoint. In an attempt to encourage abstinence before marriage and to discourage the use of artificial contraceptives, Vatican representatives claim that condoms are ineffective against pregnancy and AIDS, reports Pollitt. With the world in the midst of a deadly AIDS pandemic, such false pronouncements against condoms are immoral and deeply irrational, she concludes. Pollitt is a columnist with the *Nation*, a biweekly journal of liberal opinion.

As you read, consider the following questions:

1. In what ways can anti-condom propaganda backfire, according to Pollitt?
2. According to the author, what percentage of the population in Botswana is infected with the AIDS virus?
3. How many women die in illegal abortions each year, according to Pollitt?

There are many things to be said against condoms, and most people reading this have probably said them all. But at least they work. Not perfectly—they slip, they break, they require more forethought and finesse and cooperation and trust than is easy to bring to sex every single time, and, a major drawback in this fallen world, they place women's safety in the hands of men. But for birth control they are a whole lot better than the rhythm method or prayer or nothing, and for protection from sexually transmitted diseases they are all we have. This is not exactly a controversial statement; people have been using condoms as a barrier against disease as long as rubber has been around (indeed, before—as readers of James Boswell's journals know). You could ask a thousand doctors—ten thousand doctors—before you'd find one who said, Condoms? Don't bother.

A "Mixed Message"?

But what do doctors know? Or the Centers for Disease Control, or the World Health Organization, or the American Foundation for AIDS Research (Amfar)? These days, the experts on condoms are politicians, preachers and priests, and the word from above is: Condoms don't work. That is what students are being taught in the abstinence-only sex ed favored by the religious right and funded by the Bush administration—$117 million of your annual tax dollars at work. The theory is that even mentioning condoms, much less admitting that they dramatically reduce the chances of pregnancy or HIV infection, sends a "mixed message" about the value of total abstinence until marriage. How absurd—it's like saying that seat belts send a mixed message about the speed limit or vitamin pills send a mixed message about vegetables. Anti-condom propaganda can backfire, too: true, some kids may be scared away from sex although probably not until marriage; others, though, hear only a reason to throw caution to the winds. According to a 2002 Human Rights Watch report on abstinence-only sex ed in Texas, a condoms-don't-work ad campaign led sexually active teens to have unprotected sex: "My boyfriend says they don't work. He heard it on the radio." Why is the Bush administration giving horny teenage boys an excuse to be sexually selfish?

You might as well have high school teachers telling them using a condom during sex is like taking a shower in a raincoat.

Anti-Condom Propaganda

Now it seems the Vatican is joining fundamentalist Protestants to spread the word against condoms around the globe. "To talk of condoms as 'safe sex' is a form of Russian roulette," said Alfonso Lopez Trujillo, head of the Vatican's office on the family. On the BBC Panorama program, "Sex and the Holy City," Lopez Trujillo explained, "The AIDS virus is roughly 450 times smaller than the spermatozoon. The spermatozoon can easily pass through the 'net' that is formed by the condom." That latex has holes or pores through which HIV (or sperm) can pass is a total canard. A National Institutes of Health panel that included anti-condom advocates examined the effectiveness of condoms from just about every perspective, including strength and porosity; according to its report, released in July 2001, latex condoms are impermeable to even the smallest pathogen. Among STDs, HIV is actually the one condoms work best against. "We're all a bit stunned by Lopez Trujillo's lack of respect for scientific consensus," Dr. Judith Auerbach of Amfar, who sat on the NIH panel, told me. "Where do his numbers come from?" Is Lopez Trujillo, who even suggests putting warnings on condoms like those on cigarettes, a loose cannon such as can be found in even the best regulated bureaucracies? According to "Sex and the Holy City," in Africa, where HIV infects millions—20 percent in Kenya, 40 percent in Botswana, 34 percent in Zimbabwe—Catholic clergy, who oppose condoms as they do all contraception, are actively promoting the myth that condoms don't prevent transmission of the virus and may even spread it. *The Guardian* quotes the archbishop of Nairobi, Raphael Ndingi Nzeki, as saying: "AIDS . . . has grown so fast because of the availability of condoms." Thus is a decade of painstaking work to mainstream and normalize condom use undone by the conscious promotion of an urban legend.

The Wrong Side of History

When the Nobel Prize for Peace was awarded to Shirin Ebadi, the first ever to a Muslim woman, an Iranian and a

Catholic Opposition to Condoms

The Pope and the Vatican are deadly earnest about the inadmissibility of contraception in all its forms and in every circumstance without exception. Despite the drives throughout the world for safer sex, in successive pronouncements the Vatican has declared that it is gravely disordered for a partner suffering from AIDS to use a condom. In July 2000 Archbishop Christophe Pierre, apostolic nuncio in Uganda, where some 10 percent of the population suffer from AIDS, urged the country's youth to ignore calls to use condoms to prevent the spread of the disease. The nuncio was addressing young people on the issue in contradiction to the Uganda vice president, Speciosa Wandir Kazibwe, a medical doctor, who had criticized religious leaders who opposed the use of condoms. The same month, a priest in Brazil who had been distributing condoms as part of a one-man campaign to halt the spread of AIDS received a "letter of condemnation" from his Bishop, Claudio Hummes of Sao Paulo. Hummes said there would be further punitive actions "to correct this regrettable situation" if the missionary, who has spent twenty-two years in Brazil, does not comply with official Church teaching.

John Cornwell, *Breaking Faith*, 2001.

---

crusader for women's rights, not everyone was thrilled. What about Pope John Paul II, now [past] the twenty-fifth anniversary of his election, and possibly near death?[1] "[2003] . . . was his year," wrote David Brooks in his *New York Times* column, a hymn of praise for the pope as the defender of "the whole and the indivisible dignity of each person." A few pages over, Peter Steinfels said much the same in his religion column: "Is there any other leader who has so reshaped the political world for the better and done it peacefully?" More knowledgeable people than I can debate how much credit the pope should get for the fall of communism—I always thought it was [U.S. president] Ronald Reagan with an unintentional assist from [Soviet president Mikhail] Gorbachev plus the internal collapse of the system itself. With the crucial exception of Poland, the countries in the old Soviet bloc aren't even Roman Catholic, or are so only partially. Whatever his contribution to that historic set of events, though,

1. Pope John Paul II died on April 2, 2005.

the pope is on the wrong side of history now. Women's equality, sexual rights for all, the struggle of the individual against authoritarian religion and of course the global AIDS epidemic—the pope has been a disaster on all these crucial issues of our new century. It's all very well for David Brooks to mock those who critique the pope for his "unfashionable views on abortion," as if 78,000 women a year dying in illegal procedures around the world was just something to chat about over brie and chablis. But add it up: a priesthood as male as the Kuwaiti electorate—even altar girls may be banned soon, according to one recent news story—no divorce, no abortion, no contraception, no condom use even within a faithful marriage to prevent a deadly infection.

It's bad enough to argue that condoms are against God's will while millions die. But to maintain, falsely, that they are ineffective in order to discourage their use is truly immoral. If not insane.

Periodical Bibliography

The following articles have been selected to supplement the diverse views presented in this chapter.

John P. Beal	"Holy Communion and Unholy," *America*, June 21, 2004.
Ed Bishop	"Life Might Not Begin at Conception," *St. Louis Journalism Review*, July/August 2004.
Joseph A. Califano Jr.	"Caught Between God and Caesar," *America*, June 21, 2004.
Catholic New Times	"Gay Marriage: A Deeper Listening Needed," September 7, 2003.
William V. D'Antonio	"Church Pays Cost of Abortion Absolutism: Polarization on Issue Has Undermined Catholic Social Justice Teaching," *National Catholic Reporter*, July 2, 2004.
Kathryn Jean Lopez	"Aborting the Church: Frances Kissling and Catholics for a Free Choice," *Crisis*, April 2002.
David Masci	"Religion and Politics," *CQ Researcher*, July 30, 2004.
Colman McCarthy	"Catholics Should Obey or Go: A Liberal Backs Host-Refusing Bishops," *National Catholic Reporter*, June 18, 2004.
Leland D. Peterson	"May You Live to See Your Children's Children," *New Oxford Review*, November 2004.
Anna Quindlen	"Casting the First Stone: It Is One Thing to Preach the Teachings of the Church, Quite Another to Use the Centerpiece of the Faith as a Tool to Influence the Ballot Box," *Newsweek*, May 31, 2004.
Dennis Schnurr	"Catholics and Political Life," *Origins*, September 2, 2004.
Andrew Sullivan	"Showdown at the Communion Rail: When Bishops Threaten to Deny the Sacrament, They're Hurting the Church," *Time*, May 24, 2004.
John Vlazny	"When Catholics Vote for Pro-Choice Candidates," *Origins*, May 27, 2004.

CHAPTER 4

Should the Catholic Church Be Reformed?

Chapter Preface

On June 29, 2002, an historic event occurred on the Danube River near Passau, Germany. German theologian Ida Raming, along with six other women from Austria and Germany, were ordained as Roman Catholic priests by Archbishop Romolo Braschi of Argentina and Bishop Rafael Regelsberger of Austria. The archdiocese of Munich immediately pronounced Braschi—an ordained Catholic who had formed an alternative church—to be the charlatan leader of an underground movement. In addition, Vatican officials promptly excommunicated the seven women, formally banning them from participating in Catholic sacred rites. In response to the excommunication, Raming noted that "we had expected there would be something, but so quickly and so hard, so severe, we did not know. So it was a shock." However, she added, she and her supporters do not believe that the excommunication expressed the will of the Catholic community, because many Catholics "approve our decision and . . . women's ordination, as well."

Indeed, a high percentage of Catholics in the developed world are in favor of women's ordination: 71 percent in Spain, 67 percent in Ireland, 58 percent in Italy, and 65 percent in the United States. Moreover, in light of the recent sex abuse scandal and priest shortage in the United States, 63 percent of American Catholics believe that the laity should have a say in deciding whether women should be priests. Many of them agree with Raming, who quotes from Galatians in the New Testament as support for an inclusive attitude toward ordainment: "All baptized in Christ, you have all clothed yourselves in Christ, and there are no more distinctions between Jew or Greek, slave or free, male and female, but all of you are one in Christ Jesus." Others argue, furthermore, that female priests would provide a fresh stream of talent for a troubled church. "A clerical class that included women might help male priests . . . live in a world more like the one the rest of us inhabit," says *Newsweek* writer Jon Meacham. "The abuse scandal has underscored the priesthood's susceptibility to insularity and arrogance. A more diverse pool could let a bit more light into the sacristy, and having women as colleagues would psychologically benefit the men of the cloth."

Those who oppose women's ordination maintain that their resistance is biblically based: Since Jesus did not call any women as apostles, he established a male priesthood as a permanent custom. Moreover, as theologian George Weigel maintains, opposition to female priests does not stem from antifemale prejudice. "Maleness and femaleness are not accidents of biology; they are icons and windows into God's purposes in the world," he explains. "In the Catholic understanding, the priest makes present in his person the eternal priesthood of Jesus Christ. . . . But the idea that this is a debasement of women is just wrong—the highest, unsurpassable figure in the communion of saints, the first Christian, is Mary [the mother of Jesus], who is not a priest and who has higher powers. This is a lot more complicated and interesting than contemporary gender politics would have you believe." In Weigel's view, women are called to serve the church in ways that men—and priests—cannot.

The question of women in the Catholic priesthood will be debated for years to come because a growing number of women are seeking ordination through church authorities and alternative Catholic groups. This issue and other suggested reforms to the church are explored further in the following chapter.

"Changes should reflect democratizing tendencies found both in early church tradition/theology and in worldwide developments of the last two hundred years."

The Catholic Church Should Become More Democratic

Eugene C. Bianchi

The Catholic Church should be reformed into a more democratic institution, contends Eugene C. Bianchi in the following viewpoint. Bishops should be elected by clergy and lay persons and serve no more than ten years; moreover, the priesthood should be open to married men as well as women, and lay people should participate more fully in ministry, the author argues. A more democratic church would also be empowered to update its teachings on sexual issues and to enhance Catholic spiritual life through a renewal of meditation and contemplative prayer. Bianchi, an emeritus professor of religion at Emory University, is coeditor of *A Democratic Catholic Church*.

As you read, consider the following questions:

1. According to Bianchi, what are the three main areas that a new reform council should explore?
2. Why does the author believe that no one should be ordained a priest until the age of forty?
3. What potential in humans have Christian churches largely ignored, in Bianchi's opinion?

Eugene C. Bianchi, "If I Were Pope," *Catholic New Times*, vol. 27, November 2, 2003, p. 14. Copyright © 2003 by Catholic New Times, Inc. Reproduced by permission.

If I were elected pope, I would throw a six month party-seminar at the Vatican. We would slip off our shoes, unloosen our collars and roll-up our sleeves, bring in musicians, poets and other writers, artists of all sorts and, of course, dancers. We would eat and drink well. [Catholic writer G.K.] Chesterton's sense of Catholicism: laughter and good red wine, *benedicamus domino* (Praise the Lord). Enough of sack cloth and ashes; our theme: *nil humanum a me alienum* (Nothing human is foreign to me).

We would invite artists and dignitaries to join an early morning papal jog (or brisk walk) down the Via della Conciliazione and around Castel San Angelo (of course, we would doff ceremonial garb and use it only at ceremonies); on nicer days we would climb the Janiculum and jog around Garibaldi's equestrian monument and that of his lover. The Swiss Guard would provide color and security.

While we engage in this bodily spirituality, we would also have daily seminars on how the church could extend the vision of Vatican II's *The Church in the Modern World* in the present world context.[1] To deal with issues of poverty and injustice and war, we would hear not only from theologians and moralists, but also from the best minds in economics, commerce, politics, ecology and other disciplines; successful practitioners in these areas would join intellectuals. We would also invite the best people in conflict resolution.

Earth I Not Vatican III

After this six-month party, refreshed in body and mind, I would ask that all church leaders have their letters of resignation on my desk by 9 A.M. on the next Monday morning. Not that I would fire everybody in one fell swoop, but I would want to instill a lesson from both Jesus and Buddha that all is impermanent and that we must look to the lilies of the field who neither sow nor reap nor climb ladders of ambition.

The six month party-seminar would be preliminary to calling for a worldwide ecumenical council that would not be named Vatican III but Earth I, since it would take place

---

1. a document drafted by Vatican II, a council that convened from 1965 to 1968, that emphasized the need for modern reforms to the church

in Rome and in five other cities, representing major international venues, over a period of about six years. The new council would take up the unfinished business of Vatican II, dealing with both issues internal and external to the church. Earth I would be made up of representatives, clergy and laity, elected by the faithful in various national and regional churches. Clergy and laity would have equal powers of deliberation and voting. Representatives from all major world spiritual traditions would take an active part in Earth One.

In terms of internal church reform, Earth One would explore these three areas along others: (1) structural renewal from the top down, (2) updating of the sexual teaching of the church and (3) the enhancement of spiritual life. This numbering does not indicate levels of importance; all three areas should be tackled at once. Here are a few themes I would push as pope in dialogue with those preparing Earth I:

Democratization of the Church

In general, changes should reflect democratizing tendencies found both in early church tradition/theology and in worldwide developments of the last two hundred years. This is premised on the belief that the Holy Spirit speaks to us through the "secular" world as well as through the church.

(a) Major change and decentralization of the papal curia which would become a circle of coordinators with representatives (lay and clerical) elected from dioceses and regions around the world; revise the duties and purposes of the present Vatican Congregations with the assistance of experts in organizational design and implementation; term limits for service.

(b) Election of all bishops by the clergy and laity of their dioceses with 10 year term limits for bishops; election of the pope by representatives selected from the worldwide church (this would substitute for the present College of Cardinals which I would be abolishing in my first *motu proprio* decree as Pope Eugene I); ten year term of office for the pope; all bishops including the pope must retire at 75.

(c) The re-institution of a married priesthood as well as women priests; celibates as monks, nuns, brothers and priests would continue in their orders and explore new ways of including other laity in their work; no one would be ordained a priest until his or her 40th year after they had shown maturity in many life experiences in Christian communities (this would have a major influence on correcting the sexual abuse crisis and greatly improve the quality of the ordained ministry); priests would be trained as leaders in spirituality and pastoral service, leaving financial and other tasks to qualified laity; many lay persons would also participate fully in the spiritual ministries of the church.

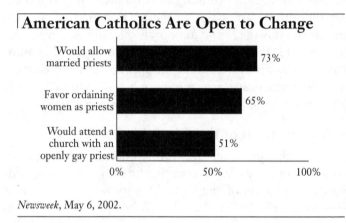

American Catholics Are Open to Change

Newsweek, May 6, 2002.

Earth I would study the lay-clerical divide that has in many instances led to undesirable clericalism; the council would renew the sense of the discipleship of equals in ministry among clergy and laity. This would require an in-depth analysis of the clergy-laity distinction regarding the spiritual ministries of the church, examining whether the priesthood as presently understood represents a true grasp of the ministries of Jesus.

(d) Local and regional churches would have much more autonomy to plan, determine and execute their gospel ministries according to their own cultural needs. Canon law would be revised to reflect these and other changes.

Revise Sexual Teaching

In light of the best scientific knowledge on human sexuality as well as insight from the key themes of Christian spirituality, Earth I would reconsider and revise the teaching of the church on all sexual topics. This would include, but not be limited to, such issues as personal sexuality, birth control, divorce, abortion and homosexuality.

Spirituality and Justice

Christian spirituality should not be seen as a category separate from all the above topics, but rather integral to, motivating and suffusing all of them.

(a) Liturgy and sacraments. Earth I would study the unfinished business of Vatican II in reforming the liturgical and sacramental life of the church. It would note both positive and negative developments since Vatican II. In general, the council would strive to adapt liturgical and sacramental forms to contemporary needs and understandings, revisiting those areas where the liturgy is still stuck in theological and philosophical worldviews of past eras, worldviews that hinder our understanding of the spirituality of Jesus and of other spiritual masters.

Modern biblical studies have improved our awareness of the religiousness of Jesus. Earth I would seek to allow creative adaptations of liturgy and sacrament to diverse cultures.

(b) Contemplative spirituality. Earth I would attempt to balance the present overemphasis on group liturgical activities in Christian worship with a restoration and extension of the contemplative life.

The council would bring together the best western and eastern teachings and practices on meditation and prayer. "Eastern" here includes not only the contemplative life of Eastern (Christian) Orthodoxy, but also of Hinduism, Buddhism and other wisdom traditions that have delved deeply into meditation and contemplative spirituality in general; for example, the Sufi mystics. Much could also be learned from various forms of ecological or nature mysticism. On the whole, the Christian churches have largely ignored the mystical potential in all humans and its development as an essential part of a rich inner life of mature holiness.

Earth I would also examine issues of peace and justice, poverty and oppression, education, human rights and ecology as noted above in the party-seminar discussion.

If I were pope, I would try to launch these ventures with lots of room for evaluation and correction along the way.

Would I also have to sleep with one eye open in the papal palace where the ghost of Lucrezia Borgia still roams?[2] And since I would happen to be a married pope, I wonder if the Vatican still has in storage the bigger bed that Lucrezia's father (Pope Alexander VI) used?

2. The illegitimate daughter of Pope Alexander VI, Lucrezia Borgia (1480–1519), allegedly committed many crimes, including incest and murder. The Borgia family, infamous for its greed and pursuit of power, produced several cardinals and popes.

"The Church is inherently a top-down, hierarchical institution. Always has been, always should be."

The Catholic Church Should Not Become More Democratic

New Oxford Review

The Catholic Church should not be democratized, argue the editors of the *New Oxford Review* in the following viewpoint. While liberals often claim that offering lay people more of a voice in decision-making processes would prevent clerical corruption, there is no evidence that an empowered laity would benefit the church, the authors contend. Protestant churches that allow congregations to select their pastors, for instance, can be challenged by conflicts that eventually lead to lawsuits, with secular lawyers and judges making decisions about religious institutions. It is neither the laity's nor the court's job to manage religious problems, the authors contend. *New Oxford Review* is a monthly journal of conservative Catholic opinion.

As you read, consider the following questions:
1. According to the authors, what kind of power struggle occurred at the Canaan Christian Missionary Baptist Church in Oakland, California?
2. Who has the ultimate responsibility for managing clerical conflicts in the Catholic Church, according to the authors?
3. In the authors' opinion, what is the "Catholic way" when it comes to discipline in the church?

New Oxford Review, "Democracy, Anyone?" *(New Oxford Notes)* vol. LXXI, January 2004, pp. 16–18. Copyright © 2004 by *New Oxford Review*. Reproduced by permission.

D emocratizing the hierarchal structure of the Church is a pet project of liberal Catholics. They can often be heard pontificating about giving the laity "a place at the table" when it comes to pastoral and even doctrinal matters, about giving the laity "a voice" when it comes to deciding the selection and tenure of priests and bishops. And the U.S. bishops have been somewhat accommodating in this regard—at least symbolically—in hearing, for example, lay testimony at their June 2002 Dallas conference . . . and in giving special audiences to both liberal and moderately conservative lay groups. . . . The clerical sex scandals have been a boon to the liberal democratizers in the Church, as ten-cent moralizers in major U.S. media outlets jump on their bandwagon. Meanwhile, the U.S. bishops are content to conduct meetings and issue soporific statements, all the while willfully ignoring the root causes of the crisis in the Church—namely, homosexuality in the priesthood and episcopate, and widespread dissent.

One Church's Battle

Against this backdrop, we perked up when reading the news report "Pastor Will Not Quit Church, Suit Says," in *The Oakland Tribune* (Oct. 23, 2003), about the power struggle going on at the Canaan Christian Missionary Baptist Church in Oakland. Back in November 2002, the Rev. Anthony Majors moved his family to Oakland from Rochester, N.Y., to take over the position of Pastor at Canaan, having received the unanimous approval of Canaan's search committee. But, according to *The Tribune*, after only six months on the job, some Canaan members "developed 'serious reservations' about the way Majors was running the church." So, during the "announcement period" at a July service, deacon Richard Herbert "tried to orchestrate a vote to sack Majors," whereupon Majors "inspired church musicians to begin playing, and members to take the microphone from Herbert and join in a din that drowned out efforts at an impromptu vote." Or, as Majors tells it, "The people who support me stood up and began to sing and pray." And the battle was on.

The next month, a general vote was taken, with reportedly 57 of the 95 Canaan members—or 60 percent—voting to terminate Majors's "employment contract." But Majors disputes the tally, claiming that the results were inflated and "don't honestly reflect the desire of the majority." "I won the vote," Majors insists. So he refuses to leave—*he won't quit the church!* "As you see, I'm still the pastor," Majors told *The Tribune.* Only now he's the pastor who's also facing a lawsuit.

The suit, brought by four Canaan members, claims that Majors has "wrongfully and unlawfully refused to vacate the pulpit," and that he has been trying to garner votes in favor of keeping him in office. He was allegedly fired for making personnel decisions "without properly consulting others in the church," which is a violation of Canaan bylaws. "Among alleged 'misconduct' by Majors," the suit alleges, "was his appointment of new members to leadership roles without confirmation by church officers."

The suit also alleges that Majors "mishandled church funds," charges he emphatically denies. "I have nothing to do with any money in this church and never have," he told *The Tribune.* "I learned coming in [that] there are two things that can get you put out of a church: money and women. So I keep my own money and my own woman."

Majors contends that members of Canaan's "old guard," upset at the changes he has made that have weakened their grip on power, are behind the lawsuit, and that the suit is based on fabrications. "I found out after installation [as pastor] the church had been split for years. It didn't surface until I began empowering other people to be part of the leadership process," he told *The Tribune.*

Empowerment?

Ah yes, "empowerment." Isn't that what democracy is all about—being part of the "leadership process"? But just who the leaders are at Canaan and whether they have a right to be there is in dispute. And although Canaan evidently has some sort of democratic process in place that allows its members' voices to be heard and heeded when making pastoral decisions, that process has been so mangled that the power to decide exactly who is entitled to take part in Canaan's "leadership process" has been relinquished to a secular civil court. If anybody's been "empowered" by all this, it certainly isn't "the people," it's the lawyers and judges.

More and more, this is the picture of democracy in action, at least as we know it in the U.S., where the courts make most of the monumental decisions, such as . . . the constitutionality of the Pledge of Allegiance in schools and the Ten Commandments on public property. Even matters of "settled law" get blown out by the courts: Want nationwide legalized abortion? Want legalized sodomy? Want "gay marriage"? *Go to the courts!* Although California voters overwhelmingly passed a "Defense of Marriage Act" in 2000, limiting marriages legally recognized in that State to unions between a man and a woman, the smart money says that that vote will be struck down in the upcoming years by decree of cavalier federal courts. In this great democracy of ours, it is clear who has ultimate power: an unelected oligarchy of judges.

Dueling Bishops

Saddled as we are in the Catholic Church with many an inept bishop, and terrorized by many a perverted priest, the ability to recall an ineffective or immoral cleric is an attractive proposition. Take, for example, the story of the battling bishops of Dallas, as reported in the June 2003 *Catholic World Report* (*CWR*). Incumbent Bishop Charles Grahmann has been making a mess of his office by protecting perverted priests—including one of the worst serial-pedophiles in U.S. Church history, Rudy Kos—and virtually emptying diocesan coffers in order to pay settlements in the tens of millions. So in January 2000 the Holy See appointed a Coadjutor Bishop, Joseph Galante, but Grahmann has refused to step down until he reaches the mandatory retirement age of 75. *He won't quit the Diocese!* Meanwhile, Bishop Galante is left flapping in the wind, realizing that with his advancing age (now 65), his window of opportunity to run a major diocese for very long is closing.

Conspicuously silent amid this hullabaloo is the Vatican, which appointed Galante back in 2000. Says Galante, "When I was appointed coadjutor, I was told that I would become bishop of Dallas in a reasonable amount of time." The six-and-a-half years Galante would be made to play backup quarterback to Grahmann until he turns 75 exceeds any measure of a "reasonable" amount of time. Needless to say, *CWR* reports that Galante "feels abandoned by the Holy See, which is reluctant to force the stubborn Bishop Grahmann to go."

Not the Laity's Job

One could easily conclude that the best solution to this Grahmann/Galante fracas would be to let the people—the parishioners of the Dallas Diocese—decide who the Bishop of *their* Diocese should be, to let them vote one of their two bishops "off the island," as it were.

Catholics Promoting Anti-Catholicism

Today the American Church is known for its internal dissension and frank disbelief. The list of organizations whose members are in full communion with the Church and call themselves Catholic, and yet promote patently anti-Catholic positions, seems endless. The causes these organizations support include homosexuality, abortion, female priests, gay and lesbian priests, divorce and re-marriage, sex outside of marriage, and a panoply of "women's issues." These organizations flatly reject the teaching authority of the Magisterium, and evidence of these organizations' influence, whether pamphlets, members, or invited speakers, can be found in virtually any parish one randomly enters. These dissenting groups didn't appear out of nowhere. They find their origin, direction, and support in the American catechetical and theological establishments. These are the academics and professional educators who shape the minds and consciences of American youngsters and adults.

Timothy P. Collins, *New Oxford Review*, June 2003.

As tempting as this may seem, it's not that simple—as the Canaan story indicates—not when there are personality conflicts, power struggles, and office politics pushing and pulling a congregation—or a diocese—in every which direction. Besides, as *CWR* suggests, Grahmann hasn't been particularly sensitive to the concerns of his parishioners. One might say he has acted as though he is beholden only unto himself. Indeed, *CWR* quotes Wick Allison, publisher of the Dallas monthly *D*, as saying that Bishop Grahmann "reneged six years ago on a deal with a group of Catholic businessmen . . . to resign." Even a recall attempt by his more prominent parishioners won't move him. Heck, he won't even take a hint from his higher-ups in Rome. *He won't quit the Diocese!* So why ever would he take a cue from his lower-downs?

Let's assume that the members of the Diocese of Dallas were able to give Grahmann the boot: It's not hard to imagine, with Grahmann jealously guarding his post in Dallas, that the democratic process would end up, as has happened at Canaan, being shucked in favor of a cantankerous lawsuit. When Majors's talks about a longstanding "split" at Canaan, he could just as easily be referring to the Dallas Diocese—or even the Catholic Church at large.

Moreover, it oughtn't be the laity's job—or, egads, the court's—to regulate wayward clerics. The laity just want to worship and pray, and witness to their Faith in their daily lives. Why would they want to be distracted by ecclesiastical politics? That's not their responsibility. Ultimately that's the Pope's responsibility. But John Paul II, despite his great strengths in other areas, has proven to be a pushover when it comes to disciplining his boys.[1]

The Catholic Way

It's always been considered the American way to take matters into our own hands (and to be suspicious of overly large or foreign bodies). But it's the Catholic way to submit one's will to that of the Church. And the Church is inherently a top-down, hierarchical institution. Always has been, always should be. Discipline must come from the top. But it looks like that won't happen until we get a Pope who won't hesitate to take stubborn or rebellious prelates out behind the woodshed. Until that time, agitation for democratizing the Church will creep ever forward, and resistance will be harder and harder to muster.

1. Pople John Paul II died on April 2, 2005.

"Male sexuality does not go away. It is not easily sublimated or integrated. It is either expressed healthily or it goes underground in a thousand different ways."

Priestly Celibacy Should Be Optional

Richard Rohr

Celibacy is a rare gift from God that demands maturity and creativity, but it should not be a requirement for the priesthood, writes Richard Rohr in the following viewpoint. Mandatory celibacy sometimes attracts men seeking to escape troubling aspects of their sexuality, Rohr points out. Celibacy would be most effective as an initiation stage of one to ten years, after which priests could discern whether they are called to lifelong celibacy or to marriage. Allowing such an option would invite more sincere spiritual seekers to the priesthood, the author maintains. Rohr, a Franciscan priest and author, is the founder of the Center for Action and Contemplation in Albuquerque, New Mexico.

As you read, consider the following questions:

1. In what way is mandatory priestly celibacy "a system set up for collapse," in Rohr's opinion?
2. According to the author, what can young males learn by going through a temporary period of celibacy?
3. What should be the church's goal as it trains seminarians, in Rohr's opinion?

The revelations [concerning the sex-abuse scandal of 2002] seem to be the beginning of the end of what some call "the myth of celibacy." It's not that male celibacy was always false or deceitful, but it was in great part an artificial construct. Men, with the best of original intentions, found out that they were not the mystics that celibacy demanded. That is exactly the point. Celibacy, at least in the male, is a most rare gift. To succeed, it demands conscious communion with God at a rather mature level, it demands many transitions and new justifications at each stage of life, and it demands a specific creative call besides. Many who have ostensibly "succeeded" at it have often, by the second half of life, actually not succeeded—in the sense of becoming a God lover, a human lover, and a happy man besides.

A System Set Up for Collapse

Practically, however, the demand for celibacy as a prerequisite for ministry is a setup for so many false takers. Not bad men, just men who are still on a journey: young men who need identity; insecure or ambitious men who need status; passionate men who need containment for their passions; men who are pleasing their pious mothers or earning their Catholic father's approval; men who think "the sacred" will prevent their feared homosexuality, their wild heterosexual hormones, or their pedophilia; men with arrested human development who seek to overcompensate by identification with a strong group; men who do not know how to relate to other people and to women in particular.

None of these are bad men; they are just on a many-staged journey, and we have provided them an attractive way-station that often seems to work—for a while. But then they go on to the next stage and find themselves trapped, searching, conflicted, split, acting out, or repressing in, and often at variance with their now public and professed image.

The process lends itself to a Jekyll-and-Hyde syndrome, even among men who are very honest and humble in other areas. The price is far too high once you have committed your life publicly and sacredly. I know how hard it continues to be for me, my closest priest friends, and many that I have counseled and confessed. Many of us stay in not because we believe the official ideology of celibacy anymore, but because we believe in our work, we love the people, and we also know God's mercy. But that loss of belief in the very ideology is at the heart of the whole problem now. We cannot prop up with law and social pressure what the Spirit does not appear to be sustaining. The substructure has collapsed. "Unless the Lord builds the house, they labor in vain who build it" (Psalm 127:1).

Add to that a rather large superstructure of ascribed status and security, and we have a system that is set up for collapse. Studies of male initiation say it is dangerous to give ascribed status to a man who has not journeyed into powerlessness. He will likely not know how to handle power, and may even abuse it, as we have now seen.

Celibacy as an Initiation Stage

In general, I think healthy male celibacy is rare, and it probably is most healthy as an "initiation" stage to attain boundaries, discipline, integrity, depth, and surrender to God. In the long run, most men, as the Buddha statues illustrate, need to have one hand touching the earth, the concrete, the physical, the material, the sexual. If they do not, the other hand usually points nowhere.

We should move ahead reaffirming our approach to grace, healing, mercy, solidarity with sinners, patience, and transformation—while also cooperating with the social system whenever there are true victims' rights to be redressed. We should do this generously, magnanimously, and repentantly.

We Catholics should also see celibacy as primarily an intense initiation course of limited (one to 10) years, much like the monks in many Asian countries. Celibacy has much to teach the young male about himself, about real passion, prayer, loving others, and his True Self in God. We dare not lose this wonderful discipline and container. (Who knows, maybe both Jesus and Paul were still in that early period of life?!) It could be a part of most Catholic seminarians' training, and during that time much personal growth could take place. Some would likely choose it as a permanent state. Most would not.

How differently the entire process of priestly formation would be configured. What a gift to the religious orders

A Burden and a Barricade

Mandatory clerical celibacy is linked to a longstanding history of ambivalence toward sexuality. Perhaps a "jewel" of the church for some, but more a burden and a barricade for others, mandatory celibacy sends a loud message to those married, sexually expressive people who feel called to priesthood but not to celibacy. The message still reads: Celibacy is a higher way of life even though, in theory, the church no longer officially teaches this. A male-only clergy is closely tied to the same ambivalence, if not hostility, toward women. Both of these issues—ambivalence toward sexuality and toward women—beg to be addressed. We will not be able to renew the church without reclaiming the goodness of sexuality and the equality of gender, and embodying both not only in our documents but in our pastoral practice.

Fran Ferder and John Heagle, *National Catholic Reporter*, May 10, 2002.

(where celibacy is essential).[1] Our precise charism would become clear, although we would surely become much smaller. What an opening to the many fine men who are attracted to a marriage partner. And what focused intensity this could give to spiritual formation during that celibacy period, instead of all of the hoop games, telling the directors what they want to hear, mental reservations, non self-knowledge, acting out, and "submarine" behavior that make many seminaries a haven for unhealth. Seminaries would not drive away sincere spiritual seekers, but would attract them. Not men looking for roles, titles, and uniforms to disguise identity, but men looking for holiness and God through which to express identity.

Steps to Maturity

Male sexuality does not go away. It is not easily sublimated or integrated. It is either expressed healthily or it goes underground in a thousand different ways. Sex is and probably always will be a central issue for most males, and it can never develop honestly inside of a "hothouse" of prearranged final conclusions.

---

1. Religious orders include specified groups that adopt vows of poverty, chastity, and obedience, and associations of monasteries. Franciscans, Benedictines, and Jesuits are examples of religious orders.

We should not be looking for a system where mistakes can never happen, but just a system that can distinguish health from unhealth and holiness from hiding. Like no other institution, the church should be the most prepared to deal with mistakes. That is our business. The steps to maturity are necessarily immature. Let's start by mentoring the good and the true, and also surrendering to that mystery of grace, forgiveness, and transformation that is our birthright as Christians. Many priests and seminarians have always done this, and I hope this gives them the courage to know why and how they are both "sons and heirs" of a true wisdom tradition. Such disciplined sons, and only such sons, have earned the authority of "fathers."

"The Church has always prospered when celibacy is honored and followed."

Priestly Celibacy Should Not Be Optional

Frank Morriss

The Catholic Church should not abolish mandatory celibacy for priests, argues Frank Morriss in the following viewpoint. Certain Christian denominations that have abandoned priestly celibacy find themselves faced with increasing immorality, Morriss contends. A celibate priesthood offers a heroic example of purity and chastity in a society permeated with lust and sexual fantasy, he maintains. Furthermore, celibacy enables priests to live out their vocation with a singleness of purpose, and such efforts forge a unique bond with God that is reserved for the pure in heart. Morriss writes for the *Wanderer*, a conservative Catholic periodical.

As you read, consider the following questions:
1. What effect would the abolishment of priestly celibacy have on marital fidelity, in Morriss's opinion?
2. In the author's view, why does the abandonment of priestly celibacy usually lead to the sinner's abandonment of the confessional?
3. What is chivalric about priestly celibacy, according to Morriss?

A dvocates of a sort of religious Darwinism—*all change is for the better*—are agitating among priests a push for making celibacy in Holy Orders a matter of personal choice. Thus in some dioceses petitions from a number of priests have asked that marriage be introduced into their ranks as a general practice for those wanting to serve at the altar and with the sacraments from a home and family, rather than in the fullest imitation possible of Christ, who as the Second Vatican Council reminds us (*Presbyterorum Ordinis*) is the Church's sole Spouse, she alone being His Bride. He was also homeless.

Celibacy and Prosperity

The cardinal argument advanced in these petitions is that there is a shortage of priests, and that clergy being allowed to marry would alleviate that condition. History, however, runs contrary to that reasoning (or is it more a quarrel with troublesome old St. Paul, who encouraged all serving the Church to imitate him, as he imitated Christ?). The fact is, celibacy never in the past was found to be the cause of the Church's lacking recruits to the priesthood. The Church has always prospered when celibacy is honored and followed; it was in the worst of times, when the priesthood itself was held cheap and dishonored, that celibacy was disregarded. It has been cast aside with practically every schism, so that those abandoning the Church herself usually begin with throwing away celibacy, as did [Martin] Luther and the English Reformers.

Now, do the ministry and priesthood of those bodies grow in any great degree because of their acceptance of marriage? Is the great rapport of Lutherans with their ministers or Anglicans with their priests because of the abandonment of celibacy? . . .

Indeed, today the Anglican priesthood with its acceptance of marriage is not only failing to prosper; it is in a condition of dissolution revealed in acceptance of things carnal beyond a married male priesthood. It is not unthinkable to believe such conditions would today be different had the Established Church not have disestablished celibacy.

Catholics, when they are presented with the argument

that ending celibacy would increase the ranks of the priest-hood, should ask themselves if, even were that so, would something more important than numbers of priests be lost, something today's culture desperately needs? That would be the example of heroism in the practice of chastity. Vatican II's *De Presbyterorum Ministerio et Vita* touches on this with an appeal to priests who have freely chosen the priesthood to appreciate celibacy as a "glorious gift that has been given them by the Father and is so clearly extolled by the Lord":

> And the more that perfect continence is considered by many people to be impossible in the world of today, so much the more humbly and perserveringly in union with the Church ought priests demand the grace of fidelity, which is never de-nied to those who ask.

The Disease of Lust

Today's culture is diseased with lust the way a human body is with cancer. Lust rots both the exterior and interior of soci-ety. Popular entertainment exposes children to sex without regard for the damage that is inevitable. The workings of lust and the structure feeding it are presented shamelessly even in private homes via television. In Hollywood's greed, the young are preyed upon with humorous or enticing por-trayals of sex. In classrooms, innocence regarding sex is stripped away in the cause of "safety" at the same age when pupils are learning their ABCs.

In this welter of filth and enervating sexual fantasy, a celi-bate priesthood and the chaste marital fidelity of husband and wife it encourages are the only two countercultural forces. Abandoning priestly celibacy would leave marital chastity without an example of heroism to encourage it, and would inevitably advance the cause of sexual libertinism, al-ready shamelessly reigning in the field of cultural exemplars.

Satan knows that real heroes in the cause of restraint of bodily appetite are among his worst enemies. In C.S. Lewis' little mockery of Hell's denizens, *The Screwtape Letters*, Un-cle Screwtape asks his nephew demon, Wormwood, "I sup-pose you've tried persuading him [Wormwood's 'patient'] that chastity is unhealthy?"

Something similar is at work now regarding celibacy.

There is a diabolical effort to convince us Catholics that refraining from marriage is not merely unhealthy for priests, but in fact is impossible. This notion rests on the lie that not having sex is unnatural, and reflects the philosophical error of humanism and naturalism. If celibacy is unnatural, the attempting of it is very dangerous. There is at least a hint in the public reaction to the abuser-priests scandal that everyone's sexuality will break out in nastiness if it is not allowed the outlet of marriage.

God's Grace

The Church knows by both experience and good reasoning that God provides the grace to do difficult good things, just as St. Paul knows that God offers no burden beyond the ability of bearing it to those who wish to serve Him well and faithfully. As for Christ's choosing at least one married (or possibly widowed) man (Peter) as an Apostle, He also said no one unwilling to leave aside wife and family (father, mother, children) for His sake was worthy of Him. If there is any literalness to that insistence of Christ, surely it should be seen in the steady movement by the Church from its beginning toward a celibate priesthood.

Celibacy and the Confessional

There is a recognizable link between abandonment of celibacy by most Christian religions and an abandonment of the confessional, with its seal of secrecy. Luther advised confessing one's sins to the neighbor next door. Perhaps he was jesting? He must have realized no sinner with an ounce of prudence would choose to confess over the backyard fence. It is known that on at least one occasion Fr. Damien shouted out his sins from a boat to his clerical superior on shipboard above him. But then Fr. Damien was heroically a priest and a servant of Christ.[1]

Confessing sins is humiliating enough when the hearer is a celibate priest. It would take more heroism than many of us have to tell them to a family man. It is a matter-of-fact

---

1. Father Damien of Molokai (1840–1889) served as a missionary to a leper colony in Hawaii. He eventually contracted leprosy and died of the disease.

Celibate Love for Christ

The reason for celibate love for Christ is celibate love for Christ. Commitment is crucial. It is the great rock out of which the lives of those who have been ordained are carved. Our loving and sexuality, celibacy and fidelity are not additions attached to commitment, but are integral to it, the radical personal qualities which give it shape. And here too there is risk. The carving will not be without cost. It may crucify us. But we are prepared to accept the consequences because the love of Christ so overwhelms us that for us there is no alternative. We can do no other. The decision to follow him controls us. We have been called to spend our lives in sacrifice and service and we have accepted. We have chosen, in Herbert McCabe's arresting phrase, "to be as possessed by love as he was." The emotion commonly may be mild, but the force of the commitment is irresistible. And sometimes something happens which takes us by surprise and stirs us.

Roderick Strange, *The Risk of Discipleship*, 2004.

---

truth that secrets between husband and wife exist only when there is nearly superhuman dedication to keeping things hidden, or a great deal of self-interest in doing so.

The Chivalry of Celibacy

Finally, there is something highly chivalric in priestly celibacy. That is, having the priest as a model of dedication to cause as was the knight in serving one master only, distracted by no other summons or answering to no other call. The chair of Galahad was reserved for him alone because, in the poet's words, "his heart was pure." Christ said something similar as to purity of heart enabling a vision of God. Taking here purity of heart to mean singleness of love, then both chivalric code and Christ the teacher can be understood as recommending celibacy as a means toward the Beatific Vision. This takes the priesthood beyond the vocation of service to others. Such vocation joined to celibacy brings God better into the sight of the inhabitants on earth, thus encouraging them to seek undimmed and unmatched enjoyment in the true home awaiting us, where there is neither marriage [nor] betrothal.

The sociology of Christianity is noble indeed, and the cause of service to others that is so strong in this age should not be demeaned or underestimated. Granting that service can be given well, and sometimes is, by those married, if it is the prime motive for the priesthood then celibacy might be seen as a penalty if demanded in priests' living of the life of goodwill toward men. But the Beatific Vision far outshines such a motive, and if single-heartedness is preparation here for such perfection beyond, then celibacy becomes the blazon of Christ's heroes. Faithful married people surely are honored in the court of Christ above. But there they, too, will give special honor to those who gave their hearts to Him in a most special way.

Catholic mothers have always given recognition to that when they gave sons to the priesthood—that is, the celibate priesthood. For such priesthood is far beyond a profession, even a noble one such as serving the spiritual and worldly needs of people. In the pride and joy of mothers of priests we can detect their intuition that those sons are among the elect who heard and heeded Christ's call, and therefore unlike the rich young man who turned away from what Christ promised with these words: "And everyone has left house, or brothers, or sisters, or father, or mother, or wife, or children, or lands, for my name's sake, shall receive a hundredfold, and shall possess life everlasting" (Matt. 19:29).

Should Christ have a priesthood that strives for anything else?

"Jesus' not choosing any women as apostles does not mean he deliberately barred them from ever becoming priests."

Women Should Be Ordained as Priests

Women's Ordination Conference

There is no reason to exclude women from the priesthood, argues the Women's Ordination Conference (WOC) in the following viewpoint. The Vatican's argument—that Jesus as a male can only be represented by ordained men—is flawed in light of the biblical precept that baptism makes all Christians equal in Christ. Moreover, the tradition of not ordaining women is based on outdated and mistaken cultural beliefs, the WOC points out. Jesus may have not had any female apostles, but this choice was based on the customs of his day and should not be seen as a reason to permanently ban women from the priesthood, the authors contend. The WOC is a U.S.-based Catholic organization that promotes ordination of women as priests and bishops into a renewed priestly ministry in the Roman Catholic Church.

As you read, consider the following questions:

1. According to the authors, what biblical passage suggests that women can represent Christ?
2. What evidence reveals that there were women priests in the early Christian church, according to the WOC?
3. Who is Ludmila Javorova, according to the authors?

Women's Ordination Conference, "Why Ordination?" www.womensordination.org, February 25, 2005. Copyright © 2005 by Womensordination.org. Reproduced by permission.

The official church does not seem to recognize that women are equal in Christ. In 1976, experts of the Pontifical Biblical Commission determined that there were no scriptural reasons preventing women's ordination. The Congregation for the Doctrine of Faith overturned the commission's judgement and instead wrote its own statement (*Inter Insigniores*, 1976) stating that women do not image Jesus who was a man; and therefore only male priests can adequately represent Christ.

Rome has closed its ears to objections and dissent from theologians, bishops, scholars and lay people and has told bishops to suppress any more discussion of the issue. The Congregation for the Doctrine of Faith said bishops should refuse ". . . any support to people who, either as individuals or as groups, defend the priestly ordination of women, whether they do so in the name of progress, of human rights, compassion or for whatever reason it may be."

In 1994 John Paul II wrote an apostolic letter (*Ordinatio Sacerdotalis*) stating that the subject of women's ordination to the priesthood is no longer open to debate. This was followed by *Ad Tuendam Fidem* (1998) and its official commentary which appears to excommunicate dissenters. However, after an outcry from the people, or perhaps dissent from bishops, the meaning of this latest edict remains somewhat unclear. J. Augustine DiNoia, OP [Order of Preachers], member of the doctrine committee of the US Conference of Bishops, stated that many are under the mistaken impression that women's ordination cannot be discussed publicly. To the contrary, DiNoia said, such debates are necessary to a fuller understanding of the gift that ordination is to the church, and would be approved by the Holy Father.

For Men Only?

The Vatican contends that Jesus did not call any women to be part of the twelve apostles and therefore he established a *permanent norm* of a male priesthood.

However, Jesus' not choosing any women as apostles does not mean he deliberately barred them from ever becoming priests. After all he left many aspects of his apostolate to the future church; the writing of the New Testament, or the abolition of slavery, not to mention the full liberation of women which is still in process. The decision not to include women among his twelve apostles says nothing about women as priests except that Jesus, as a Jewish male of his time, knew that the custom and tradition of his day did not allow women to assume leadership roles. By following the prevailing custom Jesus was not precluding a time when women, along with men, could be ordained. . . .

Rome also uses a male priesthood as the norm when it proclaims that women do not *image* the male Jesus and therefore only ordained men can adequately represent Christ. However, they ignore the fact that the priest is not signifying Christ's maleness, but rather his role as mediator. Women can, just as truly, signify Christ because they are equal in Christ.

Jesus Established a New Priesthood

Christ made women's ordination possible when he revoked the Old Testament priesthood of Aaron and brought both men and women into a new convenant; into a new priesthood through baptism.

> All of you are children of God through faith in Christ Jesus. All of you who have been baptized in Christ, have clothed yourselves in Christ. Thus there is no longer Jew nor Greek, free nor slave, male nor female. For you are all one in Christ Jesus. (Galatians 3, 27–28).

Christ abolished the priesthood of the Old Testament, removing any difference between the sacred and the profane. He did away with a priesthood founded on the holiness of certain days, places, objects or priestly lineage. No longer was the temple more holy than the market, or the sabbath the most sacred of days, nor the priest a manifestation of the divine. Jesus abolished these Old Testament distinctions. He disagreed with the Pharisees about continuing his work on the sabbath. Jesus tells us, "The sabbath was made for man, not man for the sabbath" (Mk 2, 27). When Christ died the Temple curtain, which hid the Holy of Holies, "was torn in two, from top to bottom" (Mk 15, 38). The early Christian communities understood the meaning of this. They had no churches or temples. Wherever they gathered as a community they celebrated the Eucharist. However, by the fourth century the setting aside of special places of prayer had gradually reappeared.

Likewise, Christ did away with the priesthood as a sacred tradition. In fact, Old Testament ideas of the priesthood were so foreign to Christ that he never applied the word priest to his followers or himself. He would not have wanted his followers to establish a *new sacred group* as in Old Testament times. The subsequent growth of a separate clergy class, with its sacred vestments, special status and privileges would have troubled him.

The ordination to the priesthood is a fuller participation in baptism's sacrificial and prophetic gifts. Christ replaced a priesthood based on the sacred by a priesthood based on grace; a universal priesthood shared by all the baptized. This priesthood is given through the sacrament of baptism, and baptism is the same whether for a man or a woman.

"But It's Always Been That Way"

Rome alleges that the church has always prohibited women from the priesthood. The tradition of not ordaining women was built, however, on theological and cultural beliefs that have been discredited. Just as Rome's belief in the creation of the universe in six days, or that the earth is the center of the universe are now acknowledged as untrue, so past arguments from tradition only have validity when the church possesses informed knowledge of the issue.

The church's concept of women was based on what today we know are obvious falsehoods. Whether through ignorance, lies, misogyny or lack of scientific knowledge, the church thought of women as inferior, unclean and sinful creatures lesser in every way than men. For example, the Fathers of the church used obsolete and archaic ideas to support their position that women are inadequate to be ordained, such as the notion that God created women as inferior beings, and that men were superior to women in intelligence and character. Also they used the concept that God subjected women to men as a punishment for original sin and that women were ritually unclean.

Popes made mistakes in the past despite the guidance of the Holy Spirit. They have defended doctrines and practices which have afterwards proven erroneous. Thankfully, many of these errors have been nullified by other popes or councils. Most certainly, further corrections will be forthcoming.

Early Women Priests

Those opposing the ordination of women deny any historical precedent. However, the presence of women in the priestly ministry of the early church has been ignored or denied. Giorgio Otranto, director of the Institute of Classical and Christian Studies, University of Bari, Italy, believes evidence of women priests is found in an epistle of Pope Gelasius I (late 5th century). His epistle was sent to bishops in three regions in southern Italy. One of his decrees in this epistle states, "Nevertheless we have heard to our annoyance that divine affairs have come to such a low state that women are encouraged to officiate at the sacred altars, and to take part in all matters imputed to the offices of the male sex, to which they do not belong."

This pope condemns very harshly the conduct of bishops who went against certain church canons by conferring priestly ordination on some women. He is probably referring to canons from four councils which took place within a 100 year span starting in the second half of the 4th century; the councils of Nicaea, Laodicea, Nimes and the first council of Orange. These church councils prohibited women from participating in the liturgical service in any way, or from being members of the clergy.

Professor Otranto thinks these prohibitions prove just the opposite. "If the church councils banned the ordination of women as priests or deacons that must imply that they really were ordained." Otherwise, why ban them? As Otranto says, "A law is only created to prohibit a practice if that practice is actually taking place—if only in a few communities."

He points to the presence of women priests (*presbyterae*) in the area of Tropea, in Calabria where there is an inscription from a sepulchre referring to Leta presbytera. It is dated 40 years before Gelasius' letter, a date and location that indicate she probably was one of the women to whom Gelasius was referring. In the term 'presbytera' one should see, Otranto believes, "a true and proper female priest, and not the wife of a male priest, as other scholars have held on the impulse of a Catholic historiographic tradition that has never made any concession to the female priesthood."

Another *presbytera* is recorded in an inscription on a sarcophagus in Dalmatia and bears the date of 425. The inscription reads that a plot in the cemetery of Salona was purchased from the *presbytera* Flavia Vitalia. Here a presbytera (female priest) has been invested with an official duty, which from a certain period on was appropriate to a *presbyter*.

Sharpnack. © 1994 by Joe Sharpnack. Reproduced by permission.

So far fifteen archeological inscriptions have been found that indicate ordained women. Rome maintains these women were ordained by heretical groups.

However, it is known that all of the geographical regions where these inscriptions are found were places with only orthodox Christian communities. None of the heretical groups existed in these areas. . . .

The 1948 communist takeover of then Czechoslovakia brought vast social changes. It also brought heavy persecution to Catholics who constituted 66% of a population of 16 million. Thousands of people were imprisoned for practicing their religion. Despite the threat of imprisonment, believers nourished a vibrant faith in an underground church that paralleled the government-controlled parish structure.

Bishop Felix Davidek (1921–1988), a brilliant scholar, linguist and medical doctor, was consecrated with Vatican approval to serve the underground church. When a need for sacramental ministry for women in prison emerged as a serious concern, it was clear that a male priesthood could not answer it. Davidek called a secret Synod composed of bishops, priests and laity to consider the ordination of women.

After heated debate, the decision was made to proceed. On December 28, 1970, Davidek ordained the first woman priest, Ludmila Javorova, who served as Vicar General of the underground diocese for 20 years. In 1991, Cardinal Miloslav Vlk of Prague confirmed that up to five or six women were ordained as priests, but only Ludmila has come forward.

Following Vlk's disclosure, a Women's Ordination Conference [WOC] delegation traveled to Czechoslovakia to find and meet Ludmila. At first, they were warily received, but after hours of deep exchange, were warmly welcomed by her and other representatives of the underground church who had suffered and lived in deep secrecy for so many years. On a second trip in 1996 a WOC delegation invited Ludmila to visit the United States to share her story and to hear stories of American women called to the priesthood. . . .

Ludmila Javorova's Story

Ludmila's story and that of her community is one of people being church under the most oppressive conditions. Felix Davidek, ordained a priest in 1946, was a man who recognized the danger of the communist takeover to people's spiritual, intellectual and physical lives. He acted immediately, organizing an underground university and seminary. When discovered, he was imprisoned in 1950 for fourteen years. Ludmila said that the very day he was released from prison, Davidek was busy rebuilding the system he had begun. Ludmila, a family friend since childhood, was asked to help make the necessary contacts and to assist in the rebirth of the persecuted church.

"It was an extraordinary time," Ludmila recalls. "You cannot understand. For us it was a question of survival. We feared the church would not survive."

Miraculously, Davidek and the underground church had access to the smuggled documents of Vatican Council II.[1] They built a "church community for the future" as Ludmila put it. It is remarkable that a church under such persecution, which needed to have strict security, was so determined and able to implement a model of church that was open and inclusive. Broad consultation in Synod was the hallmark of the underground church's decision-making process!

Felix Davidek led the underground church from 1970 until 1988, the year of his death, with Ludmila Javorova serving as his Vicar General during the same period. She was responsible for communication and keeping the community's records for posterity.

Valid Orders

Davidek's death came just one year before the collapse of communism in Czechoslovakia. Bishop Jan Blaha took his place as head of the diocese. In 1990, the underground church surfaced. Ludmila felt responsible to communicate to Rome what had been happening during all those underground years. Bishop Blaha alone went to Rome, however, to report on everything.

Ludmila submitted a written report, including the information on all the ordinations, but never received a reply. Ultimately, the ordinations of the women and men were declared invalid by the Vatican and both were forbidden to function, though single men were allowed to be re-ordained and the married men to be re-ordained into the Eastern Rite where marriage is allowed. The women were given no such options. Ludmila accepts that she cannot function as a priest without the official church's mandate, but she clearly maintains the validity of her orders.

Ludmila has committed herself to writing her memoirs. She believes her story and the story of the underground church must be told for the good of all the church.

1. an early 1960s council that encouraged various modern reforms to the church

"By sanitizing the sacrament of holy orders to make it fit the [feminist] agenda . . . advocates of women's ordination would wreck the very prize they pretend to covet."

Women Should Not Be Ordained as Priests

Mary Jo Anderson

Those who advocate women's ordination are defying papal arguments and rebelling against traditional teachings, argues Mary Jo Anderson in the following viewpoint. These advocates are often feminists who openly oppose the church's position on contraception, divorce, and homosexuality, the author points out. Women's ordination is not a question of equal rights, democratic choices, or secular trends, Anderson asserts. The church's infallible teaching holds that Christ as both God and man can be adequately represented only by a male priesthood, she concludes. Anderson is a contributor to *Crisis*, a monthly Catholic journal.

As you read, consider the following questions:
1. What is *Ordinatio Sacerdotalis*, according to Anderson?
2. What three strategies has former priest John Wijnagaards suggested for "reeducating" clergy and laity on women's ordination?
3. According to Elizabeth Fox-Genovese, quoted by the author, in what ways do arguments for women's ordination undermine Catholicism?

On the third Sunday of Advent in 1998, a handful of middle-aged women wearing purple ribbons clutched purple flowers as they entered St. Barnabas Cathedral in Nottingham, England. The members of Catholic Women's Ordination (CWO) had come from surrounding parishes to stand as witnesses to their hope for women priests. "At the end of Mass, we placed our fading purple flowers on the chancel steps, as a sign of our mourning for the lost and wasted gifts of women's ministry in the Catholic Church," reported a spokesman for the group.

Unconcerned by its modest numbers, CWO participated in the first W.I.S.E. (Wales, Ireland, Scotland, and England) Women's Synod in July 1999, an event inspired by the ecumenical First European Women's Synod in 1996. That same year, Austria kicked off the International Movement We Are Church (IMWAC). A band of dissident Catholics demanding women's ordination, married priests, abortion, and Church approval of homosexual liaisons, IMWAC is famous for its "storming of the Vatican" on the 25th anniversary of the Second Vatican Council. During the October 2001 Tenth Ordinary General Assembly of the Synod of Bishops, IMWAC sponsored a "shadow synod of the People of God" in Rome under the noses of the world's bishops. Their published demands included:

> No form of discrimination should be tolerated in Church leadership. All offices, including the diaconate, the ministerial priesthood, the episcopate, and the papacy, should be open to all baptized Catholics, male or female, married or single, gay or straight, young or old, those of all races, ethnic or linguistic groups.

Opposing the Pope

In Europe, South Africa, Australia, Canada, Mexico, and the United States, grassroots women's ordination groups have formed to oppose the teaching of Pope John Paul II's 1994 apostolic letter, *Ordinatio Sacerdotalis* (On Reserving the Priesthood to Men Alone). The synods and international conferences are the result of a growing coordination among the associations who insist that equality and justice for women in the Church can be met only when women are ordained. According to IMWAC sources, 40 women in Austria have completed a two-year training course for the priesthood, and Bishop Paul Iby "apologized for not being able to ordain them" but said, "Please wait and see if things change."[1]

Although the total membership of these organizations is a minute fraction of the global Catholic population, media and political pressure have frequently pushed the debate about the role of women in the Church to the front page. The perception is that the precarious health of the pope and the current popularity of rights groups offer a wide window of opportunity for leaders of the women's ordination movement. Thus in July 2001, the first-ever Women's Ordination Worldwide (WOW) conference was held in Dublin. The location was chosen in part to embarrass Dublin's cardinal, Desmond Connell, a supporter of Church teaching on the priesthood. According to sponsors, the conference "exceeded our wildest dreams."

A Former Priest's Personal Mission

WOW organizers admit that they are refining their strategy and tactics in preparation for the next pontificate. John Wijngaards, a laicized priest of the United Kingdom, addressed the WOW conference. Wijngaards explained . . . that while meeting the challenge of the women's ordination controversy may not be the first priority of the next pontificate, "it will be a catalyst to show the problems in the structure of the Church. It will be a test case. Something needs to be shaken up in the way authority approaches this question."

His presentation to WOW, "Discerning the Spirit's New Creation," argued that the ban on women priests is driven by a centuries-old prejudice that women are inferior to men. That prejudice can be best dismantled by a carefully crafted reeducation effort aimed at bishops, priests, and orthodox laity, Wijngaards said. He outlined specific strategies.

First, he said the movement for the ordination of women needs to position itself squarely in the heart of the Church. "The movement aims at transforming the whole Church

1. In June 2002, seven women were ordained as Catholic priests but were promptly excommunicated.

from within. Full participation of women in all ministries will require an overhaul of church law, of seminary training, ecclesiastical structures, pastoral practices. . . . We should not allow the movement for the ordination of women to be pushed to the fringes. . . . This is what our opponents would love to do: to get rid of us as an invasion of aliens, a secular infection, a lump that needs to be amputated."

Second, he encouraged attendees to keep discussion alive among opinion leaders in the Church. "In the Catholic Church the main opinion leaders are: bishops, priests, theologians, editors, authors, lecturers, and teachers. . . . We must promote seminars, workshops, and conferences on the ordination of women wherever possible. Organizations should be asked to devote a regular event (for instance, their annual meeting) to this topic."

Third, he said, women should be at the altar in liturgical settings. "Though the priestly ministry extends much wider than presiding over the Eucharist, it is women's closeness to the Eucharist that will serve as a powerful symbol for traditional Catholics. . . . Inclusive language should be used at all times during liturgical services.

Even if the officiating priest forgets to do this, other ministers such as readers and preachers should observe the rule. People will get the point. During the prayers of intercession, a regular petition could be inserted asking the Holy Spirit to guide the Church in the matter of the ordination of women, or some such prayer.". . .

The Dissident Celebrity

As startling as Wijngaards's open opposition to Church teachings may be for orthodox Catholics, the appearance of U.S. Benedictine Sister Joan Chittister at the WOW conference was an even greater drama. Three months before the conference, Sister Chittister's prioress, Sister Christine Vladimiroff, had been negotiating with Vatican officials over Sister Chittister's participation in an event that was clearly organized as an act of defiance against Church authorities. Chittister planned to represent the U.S.-based Women's Ordination Conference (WOC). The Vatican "ordered me to prohibit Sister Joan from attending the conference where she is a main speaker," Vladimiroff said. The prioress declined Rome's request. "I cannot be used by the Vatican to deliver an order of silencing. . . . Benedictine communities of men and women were never intended to be part of the hierarchical or clerical status of the Church," she said. . . .

Safeguarding the Tradition

Priestly ordination, which hands on the office entrusted by Christ to his Apostles of teaching, sanctifying and governing the faithful, has in the Catholic Church from the beginning always been reserved to men alone. This tradition has also been faithfully maintained by the Oriental Churches.

When the question of the ordination of women arose in the Anglican Communion, Pope Paul VI, out of fidelity to his office of safeguarding the Apostolic Tradition, and also with a view to removing a new obstacle placed in the way of Christian unity, reminded Anglicans of the position of the Catholic Church: "She holds that it is not admissible to ordain women to the priesthood, for very fundamental reasons. These reasons include: the example recorded in the Sacred Scriptures of Christ choosing his Apostles only from among men; the constant practice of the Church, which has imitated Christ in choosing only men; and her living teaching authority which has consistently held that the exclusion of women from the priesthood is in accordance with God's plan for his Church."

John Paul II, *Ordinatio Sacerdotalis*, 1994.

Sister Chittister is a familiar pillar of the American Catholic dissident movement. Soon after *Ordinatio Sacerdotalis* was issued, Mike Wallace of *60 Minutes* brought Sister Chittister into 30 million American homes. Referring to the priest shortage that WOC believes should be alleviated by ordaining women, Sister Chittister told the nation, "Faced with a choice between maleness and sacraments, the Church has chosen for maleness.". . .

Her address to those gathered at WOW was unequivocal: "They [Catholics] need what they have always needed: they need community, not patriarchal clericalism; they need the sacred, not the sexist; they need the human, not the homophobic. The people need more prophets of equality, not more pretenders to a priesthood of male privilege."

Born in the USA

Most proponents of women's ordination agree that the earliest organized efforts of the movement began in the mid-1970s in Detroit. Sister Chittister was then president of the Leadership Conference of Women Religious. The post-Vatican II upheaval in the Church emptied convents across the land. Conflict and confrontation spread within religious communities, many losing all sense of their communal identities. Legions of nuns were drawn into the "politics of confrontation"; in some cases, evangelizing for feminism seemed to supplant evangelizing for Christ.

The Congregation for the Doctrine of the Faith issued the declaration *Inter Insigniores* in October 1976 (On Admission of Women to the Priesthood): "The Catholic Church has never felt that priestly or episcopal ordination can be validly conferred on women." The declaration refuted the secular interpretation of women's ordination as a matter of democratic equality: "Thus one must note the extent to which the Church is a society different from other societies, original in her nature and in her structures. The pastoral charge in the Church is normally linked to the sacrament of Order; it is not a simple government, comparable to the modes of authority found in the States. It is not granted by people's spontaneous choice."

The rage of women who viewed themselves as persecuted by a patriarchal lock on the keys of spiritual power would not be quieted. Feminist theologians and scholars joined the fray. Much of their work is a virulent strain of rebellious self-justification, with forays into New Age, liberation theology and even occult goddess worship.

The Attitude in the Academy

Two examples from the University of Notre Dame illustrate an attitude that has become increasingly common in the academy. Elizabeth Schussler Fiorenza's *In Memory of Her* borrows from liberation theology and argues that biblical interpretation is a "political act." Fiorenza, who is now the Krister Stendahl Professor at Harvard Divinity School, taught at Notre Dame in the 1970s. She views patriarchy and androcentrism as a systemic flaw in the biblical texts.

Noted priests, too, got behind the "struggle for justice" with academic articles and books defending women's ordination. Rev. Richard McBrien of the University of Notre Dame produced *The Remaking of the Church* in 1973. McBrien offered an ingenuous rejection of the ontological defense of the male priesthood: "There is absolutely no biblical, doctrinal or theological basis for suggesting that his [Jesus'] maleness was a necessary precondition for the Incarnation."

One of the earliest radical groups to champion the "spirit of Vatican II," Women's Ordination Conference (WOC) had acquired an office and initiated liturgical protests nationwide by 1977. WOC enjoyed the guidance of the radical edge of feminist theology, which pressed the issue at every opportunity. The no-turning-back moment for many in the movement came in 1979 when Sister Teresa Kane, then-president of the Leadership Conference of Women Religious, donned a man's suit to greet Pope John Paul II during his first American tour as pope. She demanded that he permit women to be ordained. A decade later, a defiant Rev. Bill Callahan invited Sister Kane to "colead" the eucharistic prayer during a Call to Action conference liturgy.

Rosemary Radford Ruether, a champion of artificial contraception before *Humanae Vitae* (1968)[2] was promulgated, advanced WOC debates with the claim that the ordained are called from within the community, not ordained from above. Ruether is author of *Sexism and God-Talk: Toward a Feminist Theology*. She now counsels women to search inward for a God who will "level the heavens and exalt the earth.". . .

Helen Hull Hitchcock, founder and director of Women for Faith and Family, an orthodox educational organization faithful to the magisterium, says, "The feminists want an androgynous, gender-blind society. . . . You notice that they are opposite the Church on all other issues of sexual morality: celibacy, contraception, divorce, abortion, homosexuality. They say they stay in the Church because they love her, but it is the kiss of Judas."

After 18 months of debate by theologians as to the dogmatic nature of the apostolic letter *Ordinatio Sacerdotalis*,

---

2. *Humanae Vitae* reaffirmed the church's ban on artificial birth control.

Joseph Cardinal Ratzinger, head of the Congregation for the Doctrine of the Faith, wrote, "This teaching requires definitive assent. . . . It has been set forth infallibly by the ordinary and universal Magisterium."[3]

[Catholics Speak Out founder Sister Maureen] Fiedler told a National Public Radio audience that the apostolic letter and the Ratzinger clarification "is the last gasp of desperate and insecure men trying to shore up a crumbling status quo. Roman Catholic women will be ordained priests—perhaps sooner than we think." Fiedler may well believe so in part because organizations such as the Catholic Theological Society of America (CTSA) also rejected the teaching, with the claim (at its 1997 meeting) that there were among theologians "serious doubts regarding the nature of the authority of this teaching." [Then] Bernard Cardinal Law of Boston soundly thumped CTSA as "a wasteland" for its rejection of the definitive teaching.

WOW lists several points as a warrant to ordain women despite the verdict of Rome. WOW defenders cast aside the argument that "the Tradition [is] that the Church has never ordained women." They argue that the social and customary practices of the Jews militated against Jesus choosing women as apostles. Orthodox rebuttals answer that argument by enumerating the countercultural actions that Christ took on behalf of women.

Fiedler doesn't buy the theology that explains the mystery of Christ as Bridegroom to His bride, the Church, as a marital image that requires a male priest to image the donation of divine life. "Oh, that is [Father] Joe Fessio's argument. I debated him at Georgetown on that point. He is taking a lovely image and trying to make it literal. No, Christ's maleness is accidental, he is an example of a human. . . . A woman's physical organs are not the criteria for candidacy to the ordained ministry."

Christ's Maleness Is Not an Accident

Elizabeth Fox-Genovese is the author of *Feminism Is Not the Story of My Life* and Eleonore Raoul Professor of the Humanities at Emory University. Asked about the notion that

3. Joseph Ratzinger was elected as Pope Benedict XVI in 2005.

Christ's maleness was "accidental," Fox-Genovese found the idea to be "errant nonsense."

"The essence of Catholicism lies in the Eucharist, specifically the real presence in the Eucharist," she noted. "To argue that Jesus was only 'accidentally' male is precisely to attack that real presence and hence strike a dagger at the heart of the faith. But then, I strongly suspect (not to be uncharitable) that that is the whole point. One of the great beauties and strengths of the Catholic faith—in addition to its being Truth—lies in its insistence upon embodiment (an insistence that it shares with Judaism, but not Protestantism). We are both body and soul, and everything turns upon the interrelation and interdependence of the two. Thus, 'the Word was made flesh and dwelt among us'; we believe in the resurrection of the body; we believe in the real presence in the Eucharist. Arguments for women's ordination implicitly—and often explicitly—necessarily attack the foundations of Catholicism because they take the Protestant turn of arguing for the significance of symbolism over substance (or reality). This path rapidly leads away from the understanding of Christ as both God and man; it completely does away with the Blessed Mother as the Theotokis (the mother of God); and, of course, it points toward the denial of the authority of the Magisterium."

Critics of *Ordinatio Sacerdotalis* question whether proper use of authority was used by the Vatican in formulating the Church's official position on women's ordination. But this line of assault is ultimately impotent, as many dissenters themselves concede. Orthodoxy recognizes that in this matter, as in others, the Church exercises a wisdom that goes well beyond the impoverished political categories of the present age. Those who would homogenize both human sexuality and ministerial roles in search of a putative "equality" and "empowerment" for women are missing the point. By sanitizing the sacrament of holy orders to make it fit the agenda of secular feminism, advocates of women's ordination would wreck the very prize they pretend to covet. The priesthood they seem to want may not be a priesthood worth having.

Periodical Bibliography

The following articles have been selected to supplement the diverse views presented in this chapter.

Andrew R. Baker — "Ordination and Same Sex Attraction: The Best and Safest Course of Action Is Not to Admit Him to Holy Orders," *America*, September 30, 2002.

Robert J. Comiskey — "Gay, Lesbian Catholics Should Go Public and Show Up at Church," *National Catholic Reporter*, November 16, 2001.

Peter Feuerherd — "Not So Fast," *Commonweal*, January 17, 2003.

James K. Fitzpatrick — "God, the Mother, and Women Priests," *Wanderer*, August 23, 2001.

Luke Timothy Johnson — "Sex, Women, and the Church: The Need for Prophetic Change," *Catholic New Times*, January 4, 2004.

Hans Kung — "Happy to Stay in the Church; Happy to Change It," *Catholic New Times*, November 2, 2003.

David Malloy — "The Sometimes Difficult but Ultimately Postive News About Priestly Vocations," *Origins*, August 1, 2002.

Jon Meacham — "Sex and the Church: A Case for Change," *Newsweek*, May 6, 2002.

Bill Mochon — "Praying for Acceptance," *Genre*, July 2002.

James Ricci — "Memories of a 'Collapsed Catholic,'" *Los Angeles Times Magazine*, May 5, 2002.

Rosemary Radford Ruether — "Protest Ordinations Neglect Community," *National Reporter*, May 2, 2003.

Russell Shaw — "Ignoring the Obvious: The Unreality of American Catholicism," *Crisis*, March 2003.

Ann Wells — "Thoughts from a Gay Teacher in a Catholic School," *U.S. Catholic*, January 2002.

Joseph F. Wilson — "Do the Faithful Realize the Problems with Optional Celibacy?" *Wanderer*, August 28, 2003.

Carol Zaleski — "In Defense of Celibacy," *Christian Century*, May 8, 2002.

Glossary

beatification: a step in the process of proclaiming a holy person a saint, requiring evidence of a miracle brought about by prayers to the person.

bishop: a priest who serves as the pastoral leader of a diocese.

canonization: the final step in the process by which the church declares a person to be a saint.

cardinal: a member of the group that assists the pope in governing the church. Cardinals are appointed by the pope, and the college of cardinals elects new popes.

clergy: People who are ordained for sacred ministry in the church. There are three clerical ranks in the Catholic Church: deacons, priests, and bishops.

Congregation for the Doctrine of the Faith: an office of the Roman curia that is responsible for safeguarding Catholic faith and morals.

deacon: an ordained minister who preaches and who serves other teaching, counseling, or pastoral responsibilities according to local need.

diocese: a Catholic community defined by region or territory.

ecumenical council: An assembly of all Catholic bishops together with the pope to discuss questions of faith, worship, doctrine, education, and other subjects.

ecumenism: an attitude emphasizing unity among Christian churches and ultimately among all religious communities.

encyclical: A formal letter written by the pope and addressed to members of the church or to the public at large. Encyclicals typically discuss serious matters, such as morality, doctrine, peace and justice, etc.

eucharist: The sacrament of communion in which bread and wine is consecrated by a priest and shared as the body and blood of Jesus Christ.

Evangelium Vitae: The 1995 encyclical by Pope John Paul II emphasizing the sacredness of human life from conception until natural death.

excommunication: a penalty that bars a person from receiving or administering sacraments.

holy see: A term used to designate the pope as the head of the

Church and all those associated with him who assist in its administration.

Humanae Vitae: The 1968 encyclical by Pope Paul VI that reaffirmed the ban on artificial contraception.

laity (laypersons): Participating members of the church who are not clergy.

liberation theology: a theology emphasizing the emancipation of oppressed people from political and socioeconomic injustice.

liturgy: the official public prayers and rites of the church.

magisterium: the teaching authority of the church, which is vested in the pope and in the bishops together and in union with the pope.

pastor: a priest appointed to lead a specific church community.

priest: a minister who has been ordained to celebrate Mass and administer sacraments.

religious: an individual who publicly professes vows of poverty, chastity, and obedience and who joins a religious community as a brother or a sister (nun).

religious order: a specified group that adopts vows of poverty, chastity, and obedience, including communities that form monasteries. Franciscans, Benedictines, and Jesuits are examples of religious orders.

Roman curia: the governing bureaucracy of the Catholic church.

sacrament: one of the seven sacred rites of the church: baptism, confirmation, eucharist, reconciliation (confession and penance), anointing of the sick, marriage, and holy orders (priestly ordination).

synod: a gathering of church leaders to analyze and make decisions on matters of importance to the church.

Vatican: an independent state in Italy where the pope resides; a term also used to describe the central authority of the church: the pope, the Roman curia, and the Vatican city state together.

Vatican II: the Catholic Church's twenty-first ecumenical council that convened between 1962 and 1965. It consisted of a series of formal meetings and discussions among the bishops that resulted in various modern reforms to the Church.

saint: a person recognized by the church as someone who has lived a holy and heroic life and who may be publicly venerated by the faithful.

For Further Discussion

Chapter 1

1. James K. Fitzpatrick argues that the sex abuse scandals have caused lasting damage to the church because now Catholics will be less likely to accept the hierarchy's teachings on personal morality. How do you think Richard P. McBrien would respond to Fitzpatrick's contention? Support your answer with evidence from the viewpoints.

2. Daniel Jonah Goldhagen is a Jewish political scientist, author, and historian; David G. Dalin is a rabbi, author, and scholar of Christian-Jewish relations. Does knowing Goldhagen's and Dalin's religious affiliation influence your assessment of their arguments concerning the Catholic Church and the Holocaust? Explain.

3. Angela Bonavoglia maintains that the Catholic Church is ready for the reform movement that is working to make the institution more liberal and democratic. Bronwen Catherine McShea contends that younger Catholics are returning to orthodoxy and traditional church teachings. What kinds of support do these authors use to back up their arguments? Whose use of evidence is more convincing? Why?

Chapter 2

1. The viewpoints in this chapter discuss several potential causes or contributing factors underlying the sex abuse scandals in the Catholic Church. Consider each contributing factor and then list the arguments for and against linking these factors with child sexual abuse in the church. Note whether the arguments are based on facts, values, emotions, or other considerations. If you believe a suggested contributing factor should not be considered at all, explain why.

2. According to George Weigel, the sex abuse crisis in the Catholic Church has nothing to do with "authoritarianism" in the church because the church, he contends, is not an authoritarian institution. How might Larry B. Stammer respond to Weigel's argument? Use evidence from the viewpoints to defend your answer.

Chapter 3

1. Joan Chittister disagrees with bishops John Donoghue, Robert Baker, and Peter Jugis on the question of denying communion to pro-choice Catholic politicians. However, they each agree that the Catholic Church and Catholic policy makers play an impor-

tant role in the public arena. Do you believe that the Catholic Church should "lead the discussion" on moral issues in the United States? Why or why not?

2. The Congregation for the Doctrine of the Faith relies on scripture and the Catholic Catechism as a basis for opposing homosexual marriage. Why does Matthew Fox believe that scripture and tradition are poor grounds for judging the morality of homosexuality? Which author's insights do you think offer better guidance for society? Explain.

3. What do the editors of *Catholic Insight* find disturbing about the widespread acceptance of contraception? Do they offer convincing evidence to support their conclusions? Why is Katha Pollitt alarmed about the Vatican's opposition to condom use? What data does she use to bolster her argument? Which viewpoint is more compelling, in your opinion? Why?

Chapter 4

1. After reading the viewpoints by Eugene C. Bianchi and *New Oxford Review*, do you believe that "democratizing" the Catholic Church is a plausible goal? Why or why not?

2. Richard Rohr contends that celibacy should be part of a period of initiation for priests, after which they can decide to remain celibate or marry. Why does Frank Morriss disagree with Rohr's argument for optional celibacy? What does each author believe to be the purpose of priestly celibacy?

3. Before reading this chapter, what did you assume would be the Catholic stance on ordaining women as priests? Did the chapter change your understanding of the Catholic viewpoint? Explain your response.

Organizations to Contact

The editors have compiled the following list of organizations concerned with the issues debated in this book. The descriptions are derived from materials provided by the organizations. All have publications or information available for interested readers. The list was compiled on the date of publication of the present volume; names, addresses, phone and fax numbers, and e-mail and Internet addresses may change. Be aware that many organizations take several weeks or longer to respond to inquiries, so allow as much time as possible.

American Civil Liberties Union (ACLU)
125 Broad St., 18th Floor, New York, NY 10004
(212) 549-2585
Web site: www.aclu.org
The ACLU is a national organization that works to defend Americans' civil rights guaranteed in the U.S. Constitution, including rights of religious expression. It opposes excessive entanglement of church and state. Its publications include the handbook *The Right to Religious Liberty* and the semiannual newsletter *Civil Liberties Alert*.

Americans United for Separation of Church and State (AU)
518 C St. NE, Washington, DC 20002
(202) 466-3234 • fax: (202) 466-2587
e-mail: americansunited@au.org • Web site: www.au.org
AU works to protect the constitutional principle of church-state separation. It opposes mandatory prayer in public schools, tax dollars for parochial schools, and religious groups' participating in politics. AU publishes the monthly *Church & State* magazine as well as issue papers, legislative alerts, reference materials, and books.

Association for the Rights of Catholics in the Church (ARCC)
PO Box 85, Southampton, MA 01073
(413) 527-9929 • fax: (413) 527-5877
e-mail: arccangel@charter.net
Web site: www.arcc-catholic-rights.net
Founded in 1980 by lay and clerical Catholics, ARCC's primary goal is to promote accountability, institutionalize shared decision making, and preserve the rights of all Catholics. On it Web site, ARCC provides access to archives of its newsletter, the *ARCC*

Light, and documents written by ARCC members, including "Do Parishes Have Rights?" and "Gays in the Clergy: ARCC's Response to the National Review Board's Report."

Call to Action USA (CTA)

2135 W. Roscoe, Chicago, IL 60618
(773) 404-0004 • fax: (773) 404-1610
e-mail: cta@cta-usa.org • Web site: www.cta-usa.org

CTA is a Catholic movement working for equality and justice in the church and in society. An independent, national organization of over twenty-five thousand people and forty regional groups, CTA promotes a vision of a progressive, engaged Catholicism through annual conferences, publications, and joint programs with other Catholic renewal groups. CTA publishes *Call to Action News*, its newsletter covering developments in the church, and *Church-Watch*, a progress report on reforms.

Cardinal Mindszenty Foundation

P.O. Box 11321, St. Louis, MO 63105
(314) 727-6279 • fax: (314) 727-5879
e-mail: info@mindszenty.org • Web site: www.mindszenty.org

Named after Hungarian Cardinal Joseph Mindszenty (1892–1975), the foundation is a worldwide educational organization that provides information about secular attacks on faith and family values and abuses of human rights around the globe. The Cardinal Mindszenty Foundation upholds the traditional teachings of the Catholic Church and publishes a monthly newsletter, the *Mindszenty Report*.

Catholic League for Religious and Civil Rights

450 Seventh Ave., New York, NY 10123
(212) 371-3191 • fax: (212) 371-3394
Web site: www.catholicleague.org

The Catholic League is the largest Catholic civil rights organization in the United States. Motivated by the First Amendment, the Catholic League works to safeguard both the religious freedom rights and the free speech rights of Catholics whenever and wherever they are threatened. Its Web site includes an archive with links to book reviews and articles, including "The Papacy Under Attack," and "Anti-Catholicism on the Internet."

Catholics for a Free Choice (CFFC)

1436 U St. NW, Suite 301, Washington, DC 20009-3997
(202) 986-6093 • fax: (202) 332-7995
e-mail: cffc@catholicsforchoice.org
Web site: www.cath4choice.org

CFFC supports the right to legal abortion and promotes family planning to reduce the incidence of abortion and to increase women's choice in childbearing and child rearing. It publishes the bimonthly newsletter *Conscience*, the booklet *The History of Abortion in the Catholic Church*, and the brochure *You Are Not Alone.*

Dignity USA

1500 Massachusetts Ave. NW, Suite 8, Washington, DC 20005-1894
(202) 861-0017 • fax: (202) 429-9808
e-mail: info@dignityusa.org • Web site: www.dignityusa.org

Dignity USA works for full inclusion of gay, lesbian, bisexual, and trangendered persons in the life of the Catholic Church and society through education, advocacy, and support. The organization champions civil unions for same-sex couples and promotes theological reflection on same-sex marriage. Dignity's Web site includes links to recent news releases and a fact sheet on Catholicism and homosexuality

Ethics and Public Policy Center (EPPC)

1015 Fifteenth St. NW, Washington, DC, 20005
(202) 682-1200 • fax: (202) 408-0632
e-mail: Ethics@eppc.org • Web site: www.eppc.org

The Ethics and Public Policy Center was established in 1976 to clarify and reinforce the bond between the Judeo-Christian moral tradition and the public debate over domestic and foreign policy issues. Its program includes research, writing, publication, and conferences. Articles posted on the EPPC Web site include "Bishops Regaining Their Voice" and "Pro-Life Strategies."

FutureChurch

15800 Montrose Ave., Cleveland, OH 44111
(216) 228-0869 • fax: (216) 228-4872
e-mail: info@futurechurch.org • Web site: www.futurechurch.org

FutureChurch is a coalition of parish-centered Catholics who seek the full participation of all baptized Catholics in the life of the church. Maintaining that the Eucharist (holy communion) is more important to Catholic identity than celibacy or the gender of priests, FutureChurch advocates widespread discussion on the need to open ordination to all who are called to priestly ministry. Information on Futurechurch's Corpus Christi Campaign for Optional Celibacy is available on its Web site.

Human Life International (HLI)
4 Family Life, Front Royal, VA 22630-6453
(540) 635-7884 • fax: (540) 622-6247
e-mail: hli@hli.org • Web site: www.hli.org
HLI is a nonprofit organization that promotes and defends the sanctity of life and family around the world according to the teachings of the Roman Catholic Church through prayer, service, and education. HLI opposes abortion, contraception, stem-cell research, and euthanasia. Its Web site offers links to position papers and fact sheets, including "Ravages of Emergency Contraception and Abortifacients" and "'Safe Sex' and the Challenge of AIDS."

Interfaith Alliance
1331 H St. NW, 11th Floor, Washington, DC 20005
(202) 639-6370 • fax: (202) 639-6375
e-mail: tia@interfaithalliance.org
Web site: www.interfaithalliance.org
The interfaith alliance is a nonpartisan, clergy-led grassroots organization that advances a mainstream, faith-based political agenda. Its membership, which draws from more than fifty faith traditions, promotes religion as a healing and constructive force in public life. It publishes the *Light*, a quarterly newsletter.

Interfaith Sexual Trauma Institute (ISTI)
Saint John's Abbey and University, Collegeville, MN 56231
e-mail: isti@csbsju.edu • Web site: www.csbsju.edu/isti
To facilitate safe, healthy, and trustworthy communities of faith, ISTI promotes the prevention of sexual abuse, exploitation, and harassment through research and education. The institute facilitates healing for survivors, communities of faith, and offenders. ISTI also publishes books, including *Before the Fall: Preventing Pastoral Sexual Abuse* and *Recovering the Lost Self: Shame Healing for Victims of Clergy Sexual Abuse*. The *ISTI Sun* newsletter, available on its Web site, includes articles such as "Abuse of Power, Part I and II."

The Linkup: Survivors of Clergy Abuse

PO Box 429, Pewee Valley, KY 40056
(502) 241-5544 • fax: (502) 241-0031
e-mail: LinkupOffice@aol.com • Web site: www.thelinkup.org

The primary goal of the Linkup, a nondenominational organization, is to prevent clergy abuse and to empower and assist its victims to overcome its traumatic effects on their lives. The Linkup also encourages religious institutions to develop and implement responsible, accountable policies and procedures. The Linkup publishes articles, reports, and a quarterly newsletter, The *Missing Link*.

Pew Forum on Religion and Public Life

1615 L St. NW, Suite 700, Washington, DC 20036-5610
(202) 419-4550 • fax: (202) 419-4559
Web site: http://pewforum.org

The Pew Forum is a nonpartisan organization that seeks to promote a deeper understanding of issues at the intersection of religion and public affairs. It functions as both a clearinghouse, gathering and disseminating information, and as a town hall, promoting discussions of important issues where religion and politics meet. Its Web site includes links to surveys, press releases, transcripts, and reports such as *A Faith-Based Partisan Divide*.

Quixote Center

PO Box 5206, Hyattsville, MD 20782
(301) 699-0042
e-mail: quixote@quixote.org • Web site: www.quixote.org

The goal of the Quixote Center is to make the Catholic Church more just and equitable in its policies and practices. The Catholics Speak Out project of the Quixote Center encourages reform in the Roman Catholic Church. The project works toward equality and justice within the church and dialogue between the laity and hierarchy on issues of sexuality, sexual orientation, and reproduction. On its Web site, the center provides access to press releases and current issues of *Speaking Out*, the newsletter of Catholics Speak Out.

Survivors Network of Those Abused by Priests (SNAP)

PO Box 6416, Chicago, IL 60680-6416
(312) 409-2720 • fax: (314) 645-2017
Web site: www.snapnetwork.org

SNAP provides support for men and women who have been sexually abused by any clergy, including priests, brothers, nuns, deacons, and teachers. The organization provides an extensive phone network, advocacy, information, and referrals. On its Web site, SNAP provides access to stories, statements, and speeches from survivors, a discussion board, news, and information on legal issues.

United States Conference of Catholic Bishops (USCCB)
3211 Fourth St. NE, Washington, DC 20017-1194
(202) 541-3000 • (202) 541-3054
Web site: www.usccb.org
The USCCB is an assembly of the Catholic hierarchy of the United States and the U.S. Virgin Islands who jointly exercise certain pastoral functions on behalf of Christians in the United States. Its Web site includes contact information for all of the U.S. bishops and dioceses as well as links to news releases, bishops' statements, and the *Catechism of the Catholic Church*.

The Vatican
Piazza Pio XII, 4-00120 Citta del Vaticano
(06) 698-84896 • fax: (06) 698-85617
e-mail: Accoglienza@peregrinatio.va • Web site: www.vatican.va
An independent state in Italy where the pope resides, the Vatican is also a shorthand expression for the central authority of the Roman Catholic Church: the pope, the Roman Curia, and the Vatican City State together. The Vatican Web site contains homilies, letters, and encyclicals of popes since 1878, including the full texts of Paul VI's *Humanae Vitae* and John Paul II's *Evangelium Vitae*, as well as links to the Vatican library, museums, and secret archives.

Voice of the Faithful (VOTF)
PO Box 423, Newton Upper Falls, MA 02464
(617) 558-5252
Web site: www.votf.org
VOTF is a lay group formed in response to the 2002 clergy sexual abuse crisis with the aim of restoring trust between the Catholic laity and hierarchy and rebuilding the Catholic Church. The organization supports survivors and "priests of integrity" and promotes church reform that involves laity in church governance. The VOTF Web site provides access to survivor and clergy support services and articles on the child sexual abuse crisis.

Women's Ordination Conference
PO Box 2693, Fairfax, VA 22031-0693
(703) 352-1006 • fax: (703) 352-5181
e-mail: woc@womensordination.org
Web site: www.womensordination.org

The Women's Ordination Conference is a U.S.-based Catholic organization that promotes ordination of women as priests and bishops into a renewed priestly ministry in the Roman Catholic Church. It strives to eliminate all forms of discrimination in the church, advocates inclusive church structures, and affirms women's talents, gifts, and calls to ministry. Articles available on its Web site include "Impact of Catholic Feminist Dissent" and "Yes! Women Priests and Bishops in the Early Christian Community and Now!"

Bibliography of Books

Boston Globe Investigative Staff	*Betrayal: The Crisis in the Catholic Church.* Boston: Little, Brown, 2002.
Frank Bruni and Elinor Burkett	*A Gospel of Shame: Children, Sexual Abuse, and the Catholic Church.* New York: HarperPerennial, 2002.
David Carlin	*The Decline and Fall of the Catholic Church in America.* Manchester, NH: Sophia Institute Press, 2003.
James Carroll	*Constantine's Sword: The Church and the Jews.* New York: Houghton Mifflin, 2001.
Joan Chittister	*In Search of Belief.* Liguori, MO: Liguori Publications, 1999.
John Cornwell	*Breaking Faith: The Pope, the People, and the Fate of Catholicism.* New York: Viking Compass, 2001.
Donald B. Cozzens	*Sacred Silence: Denial and the Crisis in the Church.* Collegeville, MN: Liturgical Press, 2002.
Catherine Britton Fairbanks	*Hiding Behind the Collar.* Frederick, MD: Publish America, 2002.
David Gibson	*The Coming Catholic Church: How the Faithful Are Shaping a New American Catholicism.* New York: HarperCollins, 2003.
Andrew Greeley	*The Catholic Revolution: New Wine, Old Wineskins, and the Second Vatican Council.* Berkeley and Los Angeles: University of California Press, 2004.
Philip Jenkins	*The New Anti-Catholicism: The Last Acceptable Prejudice.* New York: Oxford University Press, 2003.
John Paul II	*Rise, Let Us Be on Our Way.* New York: Warner Books, 2004.
Mark D. Jordan	*The Silence of Sodom: Homosexuality in Modern Catholicism.* Chicago: University of Chicago Press, 2000.
Eugene Kennedy	*The Unhealed Wound: The Church and Human Sexuality.* New York: St. Martin's, 2001.
Hans Kung	*The Catholic Church: A Short History.* New York: Random House, 2003.
Mark S. Massa	*Anti-Catholicism in America.* New York: Crossroad Books, 2003.

Dorothea McEwan and Myra Poole — *Making All Things New.* Norwich, England: Canterbury Press, 2003.

John T. McGreevy — *Catholicism and American Freedom: A History.* New York: W.W. Norton, 2003.

Bob O'Gorman and Mary Faulkner — *The Complete Idiot's Guide to Understanding Catholicism.* Indianapolis: Alpha Books, 2003.

Thomas G. Plante, ed. — *Sin Against the Innocents: Sexual Abuse by Priests and the Role of the Catholic Church.* Westport, CT: Praeger, 2004.

John Portmann — *Sex and Prayer: Catholics in Bed and at Prayer.* New York: Palgrave Macmillan, 2003.

Michael S. Rose — *Goodbye, Good Men: How Liberals Brought Corruption into the Catholic Church.* Washington, DC: Regnery, 2002.

Jose M. Sanchez — *Pius XII and the Holocaust: Understanding the Controversy.* Washington, DC: Catholic University of America Press, 2002.

William M. Shea — *The Lion and the Lamb: Evangelicals and Catholics in America.* New York: Oxford University Press, 2004.

Peter Steinfels — *A People Adrift: The Crisis of the Roman Catholic Church in America.* New York: Simon & Schuster, 2003.

Roderick Strange — *The Risk of Discipleship: The Catholic Priest Today.* London: Darton, Longman and Todd, 2004.

Elizabeth Stuart — *Gay and Lesbian Theologies.* Burlington, VT: Ashgate, 2003.

John Trigilio and Kenneth Brighenti — *Catholicism for Dummies.* Hoboken, NJ: Wiley Publishing, 2003.

George Weigel — *The Courage to Be Catholic: Crisis, Reform, and the Future of the Church.* New York: Basic Books, 2002.

Garry Wills — *Papal Sin: Structures of Deceit.* New York: Doubleday, 2000.

Index

ABC News, 133
abortion, 124–25
    Catholic politicians supporting, should be denied communion, 127–29
        con, 133–34
    illegal, deaths from, 156
Albacete, Lorenzo, 104
Alexander VI (pope), 166
Allison, Wick, 171
Alvarez, David, 53
Always Our Children (U.S. Conference of Catholic Bishops), 86, 88
American Catholic Church
    decline in numbers of priests in, 12
    sexual abuse scandal in, 16, 72
    is causing lasting damage to the church, 19–21
        con, 26
American Freedom and Catholic Power (Blanshard), 48
Anderson, Mary Jo, 192
Anglican Church, 179
    acceptance of birth control by, 149–50
anti-Semitism, 37–38
    in Catholic doctrine, 38–39
    repudiation of, in Vatican II, 53
Augustine, Saint, 54

Bacon, Francis, 95
Baker, Robert, 126
Benedict VIII (pope), 13
Berenbaum, Michael, 54
Berlin, Frederick, 73
Bertone, Tarcisio, 79
Bianchi, Eugene C., 161
Bible, 4–5
Biema, David Van, 29
Blaha, Jan, 191
Blanshard, Paul, 48
Bonavoglia, Angela, 55
Braschi, Romulo, 62
Brooks, David, 155, 156
Bush administration, on condoms, 153

Cage, Richard, 97–98
Callahan, Bill, 198
Call to Action, 59
Carroll, Colleen, 67
Carroll, James, 42
Cassidy, Edward, 39
Catechism of the Catholic Church, 137, 138
Catholic Insight (journal), 146

Catholicism, orthodox, defense of, 68–69
    as solution to sexual abuse by priests, 81–82
Catholic New Times (newspaper), 144
Catholics
    liberal vs. traditionalist split among, 16–17, 65–99, 112–13
    opinion of
        on allowing priests to marry, 13
        on church reforms, 164
        on denial of communion to pro-choice politicians, 133
        on ordination of women, 159
        on priest sexual abuse, 97
    reasons of, for remaining in the church, 24–25
    young, are traditionalists, 66–68
Catholics for a Free Choice, 56, 62
Catholics Speak Out, 59
Catholic Theological Society of America (CTSA), 199
Catholic World Report (magazine), 80, 170, 171
celibacy, priestly
    argument against, 174–76
    church's stance on, 106
    decline in numbers of priests and, 12–13, 189
    defense of, 103–105, 180–83
    fosters sexual abuse, 94–95
        con, 108–10
    hypocrisy inherent in, 60
    origins of, 13, 102–103
    prevalence of, 117
Changing Face of the Priesthood, The (Cozzens), 75
Chesterton, G.K., 162
Chittister, Joan, 58, 130, 195, 197
    on misogyny in church, 57, 61
    on reform of church, 63
Church in the Modern World, The (Second Vatican Council), 162
Clark, Matthew, 61
Clinton, Bill, 100
Clohessy, David, 98
Coalition of Catholics and Survivors, 57
College of Cardinal, reform of, 163
Collins, Timothy P., 171
communion. *See* Eucharist
Concordat with Nazi Germany (1933), 38, 49
condoms, propaganda against use of, 153–54

Congregation for the Doctrine of the Faith, 135, 142, 185, 197
Considerations Regarding Proposals to Give Legal Recognition to Unions Between Homosexual Persons (Congregation for the Doctrine of the Faith), 142
Constitution, U.S., 124
contraception, artificial, 147
Cornwell, John, 48, 155
Corps of Reserved Priests United for Service (CORPUS), 13, 59
Courage to Be Catholic, The (Weigel), 107, 108, 111
Cozzens, Donald B., 12, 75, 118, 119
Cuenin, Walter, 58
Curtiss, Elden, 81
Czechoslovakia, underground church in, 190–91

Dalin, David G., 46
Damien of Molokai, Father, 181
D'Antonio, William, 58
Davidek, Felix, 190, 191
DeMarco, Donald, 150
De Presbyterorum Ministerio et Vita (Second Vatican Council), 180
Dezza, Paolo, 51
Dignity/USA, 59
DiNoia, J. Augustine, 185
Dolan, Jay P., 25
Donahue, William, 56
Donoghue, John, 126
Dowd, Maureen, 99
Doyle, Anne Barrett, 57
Doyle, Thomas P., 79
Dreher, Rod, 74

Eastern Rite Church, 191
Ebadi, Shirin, 154–55
Ecclesia de Eucharistia (John Paul II), 127, 128
Egan, Cardinal Edwin, 98
Eichmann, Adolf, 52
Empereur, James, 90
ephebophilia, 75, 117
Eucharist, 25–26, 200
  should be denied to politicians supporting abortion rights, 127–29
Evangelium Vitae (John Paul II), 127

Fagan, Patrick F., 147
Faulhaber, Michael, 49
Feierman, Jay, 94
Feminism Is Not the Story of My Life (Fox-Genovese), 199
Ferder, Fran, 14, 176
Fessio, Joe, 199

Fiedler, Maureen, 61, 199
Finkelhor, David, 94
Fiorenza, Elizabeth Schussler, 197
First Things (magazine), 48
Fitzgibbons, Richard, 75, 80
Fitzpatrick, James K., 18
Fleishman, Jeffrey, 27
Fox, Matthew, 141
Fox-Genovese, Elizabeth, 199
Freud, Sigmund, 148
FutureChurch, 59

Gabrilowitch, Ossip, 51
Galante, Joseph, 170, 171
Galileo Galilei, 142
Gandolfo, Castel, 52
Gaspari, Antonio, 51
Gelasius I (pope), 188
Geoghan, John, 75, 110
George, Cardinal Francis, 56
ghetto, origin of, 39
Gigante, Joe, 125
Giral, Clemence, 29
Glendon, Mary Ann, 68
Gli ebrei salvati da Pio XII (Gaspari), 51
Goldhagen, Daniel Jonah, 36, 46, 47, 51, 53, 54
Goodbye! Good Men (Rose), 77, 80
Grahmann, Charles, 170, 171
Greeley, Andrew, 77, 78–79
Guardian (newspaper), 154
Gumbleton, Thomas J., 83

Hausner, Gideon, 52
Heagle, John, 14, 176
Hebblethwaite, Peter, 33
Hee, Tony Van, 147
Herbert, Richard, 168
Hitchcock, Helen Hull, 198
Hitler, Adolf, 42, 50
Hitler's Pope (Cornwell), 48, 49
Hitler's Willing Executioners (Goldhagen), 47
homosexuality, 143
  caused sexual abuse scandal, 79–80
    con, 89–91, 119
  church teaching on, 137–38
    criticism of, 143–45
  John Paul II and, 34–35
  among priests, 72–73, 76
  sexual abuse scandal and, Vatican on, 85
Hudal, Alois, 52
Humanae Vitae (Paul VI), 112, 150
Hummes, Claudio, 155

Iby, Paul, 194
Inter Insigniores (Congregation for the

Doctrine of the Faith), 185, 197
Israel, Vatican established diplomatic
  relations with, 53

Janecki, Marcin, 30
Javorova, Ludmila, 190–91
Jenkins, Philip, 101
Jesus, 186–87, 199–200
John Paul II (pope), 27, 185, 193, 196
  on crisis in the church, 112
  funeral of, 28–30
  opposition to, among women's
    groups, 193–94
  repudiation of anti-Semitism by, 53
  response of, to sexual abuse scandal,
    34–35, 172
  on right to life, 127
  on sexuality, 33–34
  Vatican II and, 32–33
Jordan, Mark, 73
Jugis, Peter, 126

Kane, Teresa, 198
Kazibwe, Speciosa Wandir, 155
Kennedy, Eugene, 89, 97, 125
Kennedy, John F., 124, 131
Kerry, John, 124–25, 131
Khatewoda, Samman, 28
Kissling, Francis, 61
Kos, Rudy, 170

laity
  church reform and, 62–63
  should have larger role in the
    church, 159, 163–64
    con, 171–72
Law, Cardinal Bernard, 57, 199
Lewinsky, Monica, 100
Lewis, C.S., 180
liberation theology, 197
life, John Paul II on sanctity of, 34
Linkup, 60
liturgy, reforms needed in, 165
Lopez, Kathryn Jean, 67
Los Angeles Times (newspaper), 117,
  118
L'Osservatore Romano (newspaper), 50
Lucas, George, 14
Luther, Martin, 95

Maglione, Luigi, 51
Majors, Anthony, 168–69
Malthus, Thomas R., 149
Mangan, Dan, 98
Mansfield, Harvey C., 68
marriage
  Catholic teaching on, 109–10,
    136–37

gay, Catholic Church should oppose,
  137–40
  con, 143–45
Mary, 160
Mauro, Rita, 29
McBrien, Richard P., 23, 198
McCabe, Herbert, 182
McCarthy, Sarah, 92
McCloskey, John, 76
McNellis, Paul, 65
McShea, Bronwen Catherine, 64
Meacham, Jon, 159
Mendes, Guido, 50
Michelangelo, 144
Millard, C.K., 149
Mindszenty, Joszef, 113
Money, John, 94
Montero, Douglas, 98
Montini, Giovanni Battista (Paul VI),
  51
Moral Reckoning: The Role of the Catholic
  Church in the Holocaust and Its
  Unfulfilled Duty of Repair, A
  (Goldhagen), 36, 47, 48
Morgenthau, Robert, 98
Morriss, Frank, 178

National Institutes of Health (NIH),
  154
Navarro-Valls, Joaquin, 85, 119
Nazi Germany
  early anti-Jewish policies of, 40
  church's awareness of, 40–41
  popes lent legitimacy to, 38
    con, 49
Neuhaus, Richard John, 65
New Faithful: Embracing Christian
  Orthodoxy (Colleen Carroll), 67
New Oxford Review (journal), 167
New Republic (magazine), 47
New York Post (newspaper), 98
New York Times (newspaper), 155
Nicolosi, Joseph, 72, 78
Novak, Michael, 79
Nzeki, Raphael Ndingi, 154

Oakland Tribune (newspaper), 168, 169
Old Catholic Church, 61
opinion polls
  on allowing priests to marry, 13
  on church reforms, 164
  on denial of communion to pro-
    choice politicians, 133
  on ordination of women, 159
  on priest sexual abuse, 97
Opus Dei, 33
ordination
  of gays, 84–85, 164

of women
argument against, 69, 160, 199–200
debate over, is necessary, 185
origins of ban on, 187–88
support for, 159, 164, 185–91
would reduce pedophilia, 99–100
Ordinatio Sacerdotalis (John Paul II),
185, 193, 196, 198–99
Orsenigo, Cesare, 49
O'Shea, M. Lester, 109
Otranto, Giorgio, 188

Pacelli, Eugenio, 49–51
Paul, Saint, 143, 181
Paul VI (pope), 112, 150
pedophilia, 94–95, 110
Peter, Saint, 103
Pieczynski, Linda, 60
Pierre, Christophe, 155
Pius XI (pope), 38, 39, 113
Pius XII (pope), 38
efforts of, to save Jews, 51–52
was anti-Semitic, 39, 42–44
con, 50
politicians, Catholic
denying communion to pro-choice,
127–29
con, 133–34
should oppose gay marriage, 140
Pollitt, Katha, 152
Pontifical Biblical Commission, 185
priests
gay
struggle of, 86–88, 119–20
support for ordination of, 164
homosexuality among, 72–73, 76
secrecy about, 77–79
marriage for, Catholic support for,
13, 164
sexual abuse scandal and, 19–20,
89–90
sexual activity by, 60
in U.S., decline in numbers of, 12
women as, in early church, 188–90
Pudda, Daniela, 29

Ramerman, Mary, 61
Raming, Ida, 65, 159
Raoul, Eleonore, 199
Ratzinger, Cardinal Joseph (Pope
Benedict XVI), 142, 199
Rohr, Richard, 173
Roman Catholic Church, 16
anti-Semitism in, 38–39
democratization of, is needed,
163–66
con, 169–72
denial of sexual abuse scandal by, 98

impact of John Paul II on, 32–35
misogyny in, 57, 60–61
opposition to condoms by, 154–56
reforms needed in, 58–60
sexuality and, 95–96
U.S. politics and, 124–25, 131
Rooney, Dan, 93
Roosevelt, Theodore, 148
Rose, Michael S., 77
Rubino, Stephen, 75, 78
Ruether, Rosemary Radford, 198
Rychlak, Ronald J., 48, 54

Sanchez, Jose M., 50
Schenk, Chris, 63
Schulte, Bret, 16
Screwtape Letters, The (Lewis), 180
Second Vatican Council (Vatican II),
16, 162, 180
on the Eucharist, 25–26
John Paul II and, 32–33
repudiation of anti-Semitism in, 53
upheaval in the church caused by,
197
*Sexism and God-Talk: Toward a Feminist
Theology* (Ruether), 198
sexual abuse scandal, 16
celibacy fostered, 94–95
con, 105–106, 108–10
homosexuality in priesthood and,
72–73
Vatican on, 85
homosexuality in priesthood caused,
79–80
con, 89–91, 119
is causing lasting damage to the
church, 19–21
con, 26
secrecy fostered, 120–21
solutions to, 81–82, 163–64
sexuality
church teaching on, should be
revised, 164–65
con, 180–81
contraception has changed nature of,
147–48
John Paul II and, 33–35
seminaries have not addressed, 118
Sharpe, Rochelle, 16
Shaughnessy, Paul, 81
Sipe, Richard, 60, 76, 117
Smith, Al, 124, 125, 131
*Spies in the Vatican: Espionage & Intrigue
from Napoleon to the Holocaust*
(Alvarez), 53
Spiritual Direction and the Gay Person
(Empereur), 90
Spiritus Christi, 61

Stammer, Larry B., 115
Steinfels, Peter, 155
Strange, Roderick, 182
Sullivan, Andrew, 31, 76, 99, 125
Survivors Network of Those Abused
  by Priests (SNAP), 60

Talbot, Jack, 85, 91
Thomas Aquinas, Saint, 145
Trent, Council of (1545–1563), 13
Trujillo, Lopez, 154

Under His Very Windows (Zuccotti), 51
U.S. Conference of Catholic Bishops,
  86, 88
USA Today (newspaper), 97

Vatican II. *See* Second Vatican
  Council
Vitalia, Flavia, 189
Vladimiroff, Christine, 58, 195–96
Vlk, Miloslav, 190

Voice of the Faithful (VOTF), 60

Wallace, Mike, 196
Walsh, Edmund, 52
Walter, Bruno, 50–51
Wanderer (magazine), 18
Washington Post (newspaper), 133
Weigel, George, 73, 107, 113
We Remember: A Reflection on the Shoah
  (Vatican), 54
Wijngaards, John, 194–95
Witness to Hope (Weigel), 112
Wojtyla, Karol. *See* John Paul II
women
  in early church, 188–90
  see also ordination
Women-Church Convergence, 59
Women for Faith and Family, 198
Women's Ordination Conference
  (WOC), 59, 184, 194, 198

Zuccotti, Susan, 51